actresses' audition speeches

speeches

for all ages and accents

EDITED BY JEAN MARLOW   **SECOND EDITION**

A & C Black • London

To Clara Marlow 'A great teacher'

Second edition 2006
First published 1995
A & C Black Publishers Limited
38 Soho Square
London W1D 3HB
www.acblack.com

© Jean Marlow

ISBN 0-7136-7613-2

A CIP catalogue record for this book is available from the
British Library.

Typeset in 10 on 12 pt Garamond and 9 on 11pt DIN
Printed and bound in Great Britain by
Creative Print and Design (Wales), Ebbw Vale

JEAN MARLOW

Jean Marlow, L.C.S.M., a qualified speech and drama teacher (Guildhall School of Music and Drama), is also an actress and writer with many years' experience in theatre, films and television.

From her early days when she worked with a group of actors and writers at the Royal Court Theatre and came under the influence of George Devine, she has played roles as diverse as 'Mrs Ebury' in Tom Stoppard's *Dirty Linen* in the West End, 'Doll Common' in *Playhouse Creatures*, 'Mrs Turner' in the award winning film *The Little Ones*, 'Mrs Jiniwin' in the Walt Disney film *The Old Curiosity Shop*, and recently Lady Catherine de Bourgh in the stage version of *Pride and Prejudice*. She has also worked as a script reader for London Weekend Television, wrote the children's film, *Blue Doors*, co-wrote *The Horror Bee Show*, which was successfully presented at London's Arts Theatre, and *Haunting Dora* at the Theatre Royal, Margate.

She is Co-Director of The Actors' Theatre School, and it is her untiring search for suitable audition material for our students from many parts of the world, which has inspired this useful collection.

EAMONN JONES
FOUNDER DIRECTOR
THE ACTORS' THEATRE SCHOOL

contents

audition speeches

acknowledgements

I would like to say thank you to the actors, directors, playwrights, casting directors, agents and organisations who have helped me with this book, including:

Brian Schwartz, of Offstage Bookshop*, who recognised the need and inspired the work, Richard Carpenter, Rona Laurie, Don Taylor, Gerry O'Hara, Nicholas Barter, George Cuttingham, Rumu Sen-Gupta, Peter Aldersley, Beverley Andrews, Sophie Marshall, Nigel Rideout, Wyn Jones, Glenn Conroy, Keith Salberg, Margaret Hamilton, Mark Dobson, St James's Management, Geoffrey Vince, Natalie Haverstock, Charlotte Knights, Raymond Cross, Wayne Pritchett, Paul Peters, Peter Layton of the Drama Studio, London, Frances Cuka, Alan Haines, Geraldine Fitzgerald, Nicola Grier, Charlotte Atkinson, Reader Admissions Office, The British Library, Peter Irving, Library Manager, Victoria Library, Gillian Diamond, Richard Callanan, Helen Fry, Sue Parrish, Michael Hyde, Ronald Joyce and Tesni Hollands. Also my Editors, Katie Taylor and Jenny Ridout, who always remain cheerful under a pile of paperwork and permissions. And not forgetting my co-director, Eamonn Jones, without whom this book would never have been compiled, and the students themselves who tried out all these audition pieces for me.

*37 Chalk Farm Road, London NW1 8AJ. Tel. 0171-485 4996. Fax. 0171-916 8046

about auditioning

From the moment you make up your mind to become an entertainer of any kind, you will find yourself faced with the Talent Contest, the Competition, the Interview, or – the Audition. I was five when I entered for Uncle Mac's competition for 'Young Entertainers'. A wooden platform with a red and white awning was set up on the beach at Felixstowe and every day for a week I'd stood watching Uncle Mac and his troupe, in their straw hats and blazers entertaining the holiday makers. His big solo spot was 'Who Put the Oysters into Bed' and I'd learnt it by heart.

About six of us scrambled up onto the stage that afternoon and I was last but one. The winner was to be judged by volume of applause. 'Oysters' was a good choice. I was one of the youngest competitors, I knew all the words, and more importantly, I was in tune. The audience cheered when Uncle Mac brought me forward to take my bow. It was a marvellous moment. My mother was in the audience and I felt so proud. Surely I was the winner. But I hadn't bargained on the last competitor – a ragged girl of about seven with a dirty face. She climbed slowly up the wooden steps, took one look at the audience and then burst into tears. The applause was tumultuous. She was the winner and she'd done nothing at all – just opened her mouth and bawled. I couldn't believe it. I was stunned – bewildered. Looking back I can understand why she got the sympathy of the audience and the prize, but at the time there was no consoling a five year old who felt she had been unfairly treated!

How many actors and actresses have expressed that same sense of bewilderment after being turned down at an audition. 'I thought I'd done so well . . . they liked my speeches, I know they did . . . I even got a laugh in that comedy bit . . . What went wrong?' or students trying to get into drama school, 'Five auditions and I've failed every one . . .' or 'One more to go, but I expect I'll fail that too!'

you haven't failed

You haven't failed. You simply weren't selected. An audition isn't an examination or some sort of test to see who gets the highest marks. It may not always seem fair – life isn't fair – but very often you weren't what they were looking for. You didn't fit the bill.

A Musical Director who has sat through many auditions for West End musicals confirmed this. If someone walks onto the stage and they are not what the director is looking for, they will be politely sent away with a 'Thank you, we'll let you know'. The next artist may not perform so well, but if they look 'right' will very often get a recall.

A director is just as anxious to cast the right person as you are to get the job, particularly if he is involved with a whole season of plays. Does this actor look old enough? Should he resemble the actor playing his father? Will there be suitable parts for him in the next three productions? Should we look for a 'name' instead? It is not always the best actor or actress that gets the part – how can it be?

All the more reason to throw the word 'failure' out of your vocabulary. It took me many years and many, many auditions to conquer that feeling of rejection and realise that however good you are, or think you are, there are sometimes other influences, considerations, or circumstances beyond your control. The ragged child lurking around the corner, the television 'name' who will put 'bums on seats', or even the actor who has worked for the company before – a director may feel happier with an actor he knows. Providing you have worked hard and done your very best to prepare for your audition, you haven't failed, on the contrary, you've added to your experience and may even be remembered for next time. But let's have a look at the first audition most of us encounter when we consider 'going into the theatre' – the drama school audition.

applying and auditioning for drama school

You want to become an actor and you've decided, quite rightly in most cases, that the best way to go about it is to apply for drama school. You've contacted the various schools and asked them to send you a prospectus and application form. The prospectus should give you some idea of the courses offered and explain what will be required of you at the audition. Most drama schools in Great Britain are expensive and it is best to make sure you can afford the school of your choice before sending back your form and audition fee. Not all local councils, or in the case of students from overseas, governments, are prepared to assist you these days. One student was told by his council that they could train five engineers with the money it takes to send a single actor to drama school. Never mind. A few schools are now offering degree courses

(BA Drama), and councils are inclined to look more favourably on these. You will also find some universities offering drama courses (BA Drama), but many of these are mainly academic.

In the United States there are very few vocational drama schools, such as the Royal Academy of Dramatic Art (RADA), or the Guildhall School of Music and Drama in London. Perhaps the equivalent would be The Juilliard School or The American Academy of Dramatic Arts in New York. Most drama courses are affiliated to universities, such as Yale, and are again very expensive. There are no grants available but you may qualify for a student loan. If you elect to go to drama school there are scholarships you can apply for, or you could approach one of the various Foundations for a theatre bursary.

When you have selected the school that has the most to offer *you* and you have sent in your fee and application form, do make sure that you have read the audition requirements thoroughly. You really should apply for more than one school as you rarely get accepted on a first audition, although it has been known. Audition speeches get better the more they are performed and there is no doubt about it, you develop a way of handling auditions. At your second attempt you will not be nearly so nervous and you'll begin to look around you and compare notes with others who are experiencing the same thing as yourself. Your first couple of auditions should, I think, be treated as a learning process.

Most schools require you to perform two contrasting speeches of about three minutes each, one of these usually to be a classic such as Shakespeare, Jacobean or Restoration – and the other a modem piece (in the United States they tend to lay less emphasis on Shakespeare), a song, some movement and improvisation. A few ask for *three* prepared speeches, although they may not always want to hear the third, and others send out a list of about ten speeches, ask you to pick out one or sometimes two of them, and contrast these with a piece of your own choice. All the speeches, and of course the song, have to be learnt by heart. It is amazing how many applicants think all they have to do is to stand up and read everything!

choosing a suitable audition piece

Choose a character that is near to your own age and experience, unless of course you feel you have a particular talent or liking for playing older or younger parts convincingly. If your character comes from a particular region, or indeed from another country, are you capable of adopting the necessary accent? There is nothing worse than a poor attempt to sound like a Londoner, for instance, or a New Yorker. You may even find – horror of horrors – that the auditioner comes from there!

contrast

Contrast is an important word in the theatre. Contrast keeps an audience from being bored – and hopefully an auditioner. Look again at those audition requirements and you will see the word 'contrast'. Contrast your speeches. If you have already selected something dramatic, contrast it with a comedy. If one of your speeches is Standard English or American, look for something with a different accent.

One of my students, Tina, was born in Yorkshire of South African parents, but had been sent to school in London. She has good Standard English, which she used for her Shakespeare selection – 'Isabella' from *Measure For Measure*, and her mother helped her with a South African accent for 'Hester' in Athol Fugard's *Hello and Goodbye*. She gained places in two drama schools.

If English is not your native tongue, there are speeches in this book that cover a wide range of accents. The young black South African girl in *Have You Seen Zandile?*, and the young wife in *In the Bag*, set in modern Beijing, among many others. There are also plays translated into English, such as Henrik Ibsen's *The Lady from the Sea*, where students from abroad can often find some affinity with a character and its speech rhythms. Marjo, a student from Finland, finds an affinity with Chekhov's characters and is a splendid 'Sasha' in *Ivanov*. She has also chosen a suitable Shakespeare character, 'Phebe' in *As You Like It* – how marvellously Shakespeare lends itself to all types and nationalities – and then contrasts these with a very moving 'Sophie' from Tom Stoppard's *Artist Descending a Staircase*.

accents and ages

At the top left-hand side of each preface to the speeches, I have put the nationality of the character and/or if they have a regional accent. I have also mentioned where a play has been translated into English, or is set in a non-English speaking country. But please note, that although these plays have excellent speeches for overseas actors who perhaps still retain some of their native accent or speech rhythms, it is not a good idea for British or American actors to perform them in 'funny foreign voices'. As a general rule, you should only use a foreign accent if it says so in the script, or if your character is 'foreign' to the other characters in the play.

Underneath nationality/regional accent etc. I have indicated the age

4

of the character. Some playwrights are specific about age, others give no indication whatsoever. In these cases I have simply put 'young', 'middle-aged', 'elderly' or 'old'. 'Young' is the most difficult to define, as it can mean anything from late teens to late 30s, or even 40 – if you consider '40' as still young! It is important to be absolutely honest with yourself about your 'playing age'. Occasionally young people are able to play a lot older than their actual age, and make quite a feature of this, and I have known small 35 year olds to play children of 12 or 13.

read the play

I cannot over-emphasise the importance of *reading the play*. You owe it to the playwright and to yourself. A student once said to me that she couldn't see the point of this. The character she was playing was obviously a young American girl talking to a crowd of people – it said so in the preface to the audition piece. What else did she need to know? 'But who is she speaking to?' I asked. 'Does it matter?' she replied. Of course it matters. It matters very much indeed. Your attitude to the character or characters you are speaking to alters according to the sort of people they are, their motives and your motives for speaking to them. Are they friends or enemies? People you love, people you hate, or people you are indifferent to? What has happened in the previous scene? What has just been said that makes you react in a particular way? If you don't know the question, how can you possibly answer? Paulina's speech in *Death and the Maiden* begins with the line, 'When I heard his voice last night . . .' Whose voice is she talking about and who is she talking to? Although I have given you some indication in the preface to this speech, it is vital to find out more about Paulina and her relationship with her husband and her victim.

You need to read and re-read the play. Gather as much information as you can about your character and ask yourself:

1) what does your character say about herself?
2) what does she think about the other characters in the play?
3) what do they think of her?
4) what has happened in the previous scene?
5) what does your character want
    (a) in this particular scene?
    (b) throughout the play?

Each character is making a journey. At what stage of the journey are you when you are making your speech?

Sometimes, of course, the information given in the play is not sufficient and you may need to research further. For example, Philippa was playing 'Lena' – the South African Cape Coloured woman in Athol Fugard's *Boesman and Lena*. The character is beautifully drawn, but Philippa not only worked on perfecting the accent, but realised the need to find out more about Cape Coloured people and study an older woman's movement. Her performance was a joy to watch.

You can make some unfortunate mistakes at an audition if you haven't read the play. Alison had a recall for drama school and was performing one of their set pieces – a speech of Mistress Quickly's from Shakespeare's *King Henry IV, Part II*. When she finished she was asked what had happened in the previous scene, and what had the character, Falstaff, just said to her. She didn't know, and had to confess that she hadn't read the play. What a pity! She had worked so hard and then let herself down on something so obvious.

Ian was asked to learn a classical piece and hastily picked out the first small speech he came across in the family's *Complete Works of Shakespeare*. It wasn't until a week after his unsuccessful audition that he realised he'd selected 'Julia' from *Two Gentlemen of Verona*.

If you are plumpish and over 30 it is not a good idea to pick out 'First Fairy' from *A Midsummer Night's Dream*. Believe me, I have seen this happen. The lady in question had learnt the speech when she was at school and hadn't bothered to find out where it came from or who was saying it!

if a play is out of print

If the audition piece you have chosen happens to be in a play that is out of print and there are no copies available in bookshops or local libraries, what do you do? The Victoria Library, Westminster, London has a very wide selection of published plays, and failing this, the British Library can be extremely helpful, 'application is open to anyone who needs to see material not readily available elsewhere'. For further details ring 020 7412 7000. Material may take several days to retrieve if it is not housed on site. The equivalent of the British Library in the United States would be the Library of Congress in Washington.

if the speech you have chosen is too long

The majority of speeches in this book are between three and four minutes in length – an acceptable time for most auditions. However, there are occasions when you are specifically required to limit your time to two or even one and a half minutes. If you go over this time you are liable to be stopped before you get to the end, and if you rush it you will spoil your performance. Be bold. Cut it down to the required length. This is not nearly as difficult as it may seem. For example, 'Lena's' speech from *Boesman and Lena* cuts neatly into two halves and 'Mary's' speech from *Rutherford and Son* can be pruned considerably. If a speech does not reduce easily, or you feel that by cutting it you will lose sense or quality, have a look through the play. The character may well have another speech lasting only a minute and a half.

if your speech has lines of other characters included

In some speeches lines of characters other than your own have had to be kept in. These additional lines should of course be omitted in performance. There are also instances in these same speeches where you may need to leave out a word like 'yes' or even a short sentence if it sounds obviously like a response to a question from another character.

the song

Many students ignore this section of audition requirements, 'I don't want to be a singer, so why should I bother?' The auditioner usually insists that they do something and they proudly tell you that they stood up and sang 'Three Blind Mice' or the National Anthem. You are often required to sing in plays today, and in the United States, this part of your training is an essential. Even if you haven't a very good voice, the auditioner will appreciate that at least you made an effort. It is worth investing in a few singing lessons. Find a song that is easy to sing unaccompanied – you rarely have anyone to play for you at these auditions – and ask your teacher or pianist to put it on tape. At least you will be able to practise it in a comfortable key.

improvisation

Some people find this very frightening indeed. I knew two students who passed their first auditions with flying colours, but on the recalls froze when it came to improvisation. There are many drama groups and workshops that make a speciality of 'impro', performing professionally in small theatres or pub venues and often inviting their more advanced students to participate. If you have never done any improvisation you would be well advised to join one of these groups. They can be contacted through theatre listings.

what do I wear?

Most schools tell you what to wear for an audition, particularly if they are starting with some sort of warm-up or movement session. The main thing is to be comfortable. If you know there is going to be movement and improvisation, wear something casual – tights, jeans and jazz shoes (the ones with the small heels) are easy to work in. Trainers can be a bit clumsy. I think women should change into skirts when they are performing their speeches, unless the character would be wearing trousers or jeans. It is best to put on a long practice skirt for classical speeches. You can always slip it on over your other clothes. It makes the movement easier and prevents you from taking great long strides, as we all tend to do when we wear trousers. A change of shoes can also be a good idea. A pair of heels can add that extra dimension to a sophisticated or indeed a 'tarty' character.

should you have coaching?

A lot of drama schools say, 'no', they don't want to see a carefully drilled performance and I agree with them. However, I do think you need some help or advice from a trusted, experienced, actor or teacher. I spoke to a student who did Romeo's final speech at his very first audition. He told me that when he was supposed to 'die' he didn't know what to do, so he crawled away and ended up under the auditioners' desk. 'It was very embarrassing,' he said, 'with them both looking down at me lying by their feet.'

how competitive is it to get into drama school and what are auditioners looking for?

The Royal Academy of Dramatic Art (RADA) auditions between 1400 and 1500 students a year for 30 available places. The Principal, Nicholas Barter, looks particularly for commitment and trainability when auditioning younger (18 year old) students, not just those with nice middleclass voices and a few acting medals taken at school. He is also interested in older applicants (middle to late 20s, up to 30 years of age), some of whom have perhaps done drama at university, been a member of the local youth theatre, or worked with amateur companies, are prepared to re-evaluate their previous work and are open to being trained for a serious career.

Nicholas Barter commented,

> 'We aim to encourage initiative and develop individuality, not turn out RADA clones. My predecessor, Oliver Neville, used to say, "We are more interested in someone putting on a play in their front room, using their mother's curtains, than someone with a more formal background."'

I asked Rona Laurie, well known drama coach and experienced audi tioner, what she looked for when auditioning or interviewing students applying for drama school.

> 'The first thing I look for is commitment. I ask them "Do you want to learn to act, or do you want to be famous?" If the answer is, "Both," well and good. If it is, "I want to be famous," I know they are not what we are looking for. The second question is, "Would you be happy doing anything else?" A strong "No" indicates a sense of dedication. I was once directing a group of drama students of which one was obviously lacking in concentration and interest. "What made you want to go to drama school?" I asked. The answer was, "I thought I'd give it a whirl." Consternation among the rest of the group.
>
> I look for vitality in the work and something in the personality which arrests attention. Academic qualifications are not always necessary. Do you have to have brains to act? Not if you can act. There are "naturals" who seem to be able to act instinctively. But on the whole a sound academic background is an advantage. I am always impressed by the determination of students to succeed despite numerous disappointments at auditions.'

I then asked George Cuttingham, former President of the American Academy of Dramatic Arts in New York, the same question I'd asked Rona Laurie. His response was that,

> 'The overall policy at AADA is to admit all individuals who seem qualified artistically and academically, as well as in terms of maturity and

motivation, to undertake a rigorous conservatory program of professional training.

In the audition/interview, special attention is given to the quality of
the applicant's instinctive emotional connection to the audition material.

Since good listening is so fundamental to good acting, AADA notes
how well the applicant listens in the "real-world" context of the interview.

Other criteria include sensitivity, sense of language, sense of humour,
vitality, presence, vocal quality, cultural interests and a realistic sense of
self and the challenge involved in pursuing an acting career.'

auditioning for theatre, films, television and radio

After you have completed your drama course the auditioning process
continues. Although, hopefully, part of your acting life will be spent
working in films and television, it should be stressed that the most
successful actors and actresses are generally those who have had a good
drama school training and/or theatre experience. Of course there are
exceptions to this. Models have been given leads in films and recently
a casting director interviewed in a magazine, described how she had discovered a marvellous looking young man outside a coffee house and
asked him if he would be interested in playing the lead in a film she was
casting. And we all know of a certain television series that was cast with
a high proportion of non-professional actors!

However, if you have had a solid stage training, have worked on your
voice and movement, and had the opportunity of developing various
characters and learning to play opposite other actors without falling over
the furniture, you stand a better chance of gaining professional employ-
ment and staying in the 'business'. Even from a practical point of view,
at the end of your drama school training you will be performing in front
of agents and casting directors in your final productions, and stand a
chance of being selected for representation or given the opportunity of
auditioning for a professional theatre company. Offers of film or television work usually come because someone has seen you performing on
stage in the first place. Very few film and television directors are going
to take a risk on casting a young actor or actress, even in a small part,
with no experience whatsoever – and the easiest way to gain this experience is via drama school and/or the theatre.

'Getting a start' can be a major problem, but by now you should have a fairly wide range of audition speeches, gathered together over your two or three years as a student.

Auditions for professional actors can be divided very roughly into four categories:

1) theatre – including musical theatre
2) films or films for television
3) television and television commercials, videos etc.
4) radio – including radio commercials and voice-overs.

theatre

Your very first audition could well be for a repertory or summer stock company, where a different play is presented every two or three weeks, sometimes monthly and in a few rare exceptions, weekly. You will usually be expected to prepare two contrasting speeches, so the director can get some idea of your range of work. Find out what plays are listed for the season. If it is a small company putting on *Rutherford and Son* or *Breezeblock Park* it is pointless giving them a piece of Shakespeare or a speech from George Bernard Shaw. Try to suit their requirements and choose two modern pieces – one comedy and one drama, with perhaps an accent to show your versatility. If you are auditioning for a company presenting plays in repertoire, i.e. plays that are rehearsed and then performed for a short while only, changed and then brought back again, the same thing applies. (London, of course, capitalises on this system with the Royal National and Royal Shakespeare companies planning their programmes so that tourists and visitors can see as many as four plays within a fortnight.)

Be warned! it is important to keep your audition selections 'brushed up' – or at least go over the words every now and then. Many of these companies expect actors to be able to audition at a moment's notice. A company looking for actors for *The Bacchae* expected a piece of Greek tragedy prepared in two days, and it's not unknown for a certain well-known company to telephone you at five in the afternoon and ask you to come in and perform a piece of Shakespeare the next day!

Frequently an actor or actress is called upon to audition for a specific part in one specific production. It could be a tour, a play coming into the West End of London, or in the States – a Broadway or off-Broadway production. This is an entirely different sort of audition, where suitability often counts more than capability. You are not likely to be asked to play the 'Witch of Edmonton' if you are only 23, or 'Hermia' in

A Midsummer Night's Dream if you are five foot ten, and most 'Falstaffs' are large in stature. You will almost certainly be asked to 'read' or 'sight-read' and will be judged initially on your suitability for the part, i.e. age, appearance, build, voice-range etc.

a word about 'reading' or 'sight-reading'

In theatre, films, television or radio, being asked to 'read' or 'sight-read' for a part are one and the same thing. It means that you will be given a script to read that you have never seen before and be expected to give some sort of reasonable performance, or at least a good indication of how you would play the part. You may be given a few minutes to look through it, but sometimes you only have time for a quick glance and then have to begin 'reading'. You should try to look up from the page as much as possible, so that the auditioner can see your face and also so that the words are 'lifted' from the page, rather than looking down all the time and mumbling into your script. 'Sight-reading' is a skill that can be learnt and practised until you can eventually hold a line, or part of a line, in your head and look up where appropriate, instead of being hampered by having to look down all the time.

Fringe theatre in this country, and off off-Broadway in the United States, has proliferated as many commercial and subsidised companies have had to close down. Most of these operate in pub theatres or in small arts centres. Several are experimental and of a very high standard indeed, but unfortunately not well funded, and 'profit share' has become a euphemism, with rare exceptions, for 'no money for the cast'. However, it gives actors and actresses who are not working a chance to be seen by directors and casting directors, and there is considerable competition for some of the better parts. Mostly, as in paid theatre, you will be required to 'read' and sometimes even asked to prepare a classical or modern speech.

Musical auditions can be a daunting prospect. In the United States, actors are expected to be 'all-rounders' – equipped for both musicals and 'straight' theatre. In the United Kingdom we tend to divide ourselves into those who do musicals because they can sing and/or 'move' and those who only do straight plays because they can't, or don't want to! Nowadays, more and more plays require actors who can do both, and it is a good idea to take a few singing lessons, add a couple of songs to your repertoire and perhaps even learn a few dance steps.

films

A film director looks for a much smaller-scale performance, and very often you won't even be considered unless you are very near to, or 'are', the character he is looking for. At a first interview you may be asked to 'read' and then perhaps 'read' again on video. The director will usually ask an actor to do 'less' not 'more', and sometimes it can be difficult to adjust to this if you have been working consistently in the theatre giving a much broader performance i.e. using more voice, more movement and bigger gestures. If you are called back, try to learn the lines so that you don't have to keep looking down at the script, or better still, not look at it at all. As you get closer to getting the part, watch that you don't tense up. Relaxation now becomes of prime importance. Enjoy playing the scene and forget how much you want the part – keep it loose and relaxed.

television

You will more than likely be expected to 'read' at a television audition, unless the director and casting director already know your work. As with films, you are mostly required to scale down your performance. Don't be hurried into a reading. Ask if you can have at least a minute to look through the part. Very often you will be given a script to take away and study and come back again a few days later. Here again, suitability counts more than capability, and you are sometimes only cast because you come from that area or part of the world where the action is set. This is particularly so with documentaries, or dramatisations of crime, reports, etc.

commercials

It has been said that the success rate for 'Commercial Auditions' is about one in 20. Advertisers like to have lots of actors to choose from, so it's as well to bear this in mind and not be too down-hearted if you don't come away with the job! When you arrive for your appointment you will most likely be handed a script or story line and asked to study it in the waiting room until called. If you have lines to say, try to familiarise yourself with them as much as possible. You will almost certainly be videoed, and remember your face is important – not the top of your head. These auditions can be a bizarre experience. Some years ago a friend of mine was 'put up' for an egg commercial. She was shown into a large boardroom with a long polished table, around which sat the production team and the advertisers. There was a pair of flippers on the table and she was asked to put these on and jump around the room saying, 'I'm an egg chick. Eggs are cheap this week.' Yes, actors have to be prepared for anything!

radio

For commercial recordings and voice-overs, either on television or radio, you will be asked to 'read' – sometimes in an office, or in a small sound studio in front of a microphone. It may be for a specific job, or a general audition where your tape is then filed for future reference and played through when the company are looking for a particular voice for a particular production.

If you are auditioning for BBC Radio Drama, you are required to present two, preferably contrasting, speeches of about a minute each. Auditions are always held in a studio in front of a microphone, with either one or two drama producers listening to you in the sound box. You will be given approximately five minutes on tape and should use some of this time to give short examples of accents and dialects in order to show your versatility, although this is not obligatory. These have to be good, as if YOU slip up on an accent on radio, it can be so horribly obvious.

what auditioners look for

Who are the people who audition you for professional work in theatre, films, television and radio? They may be casting directors, producers, directors, assistant directors, writers – or even a combination of all these people. Usually a casting director calls you to an audition because he or she knows you, or knows of your work, you have written in and your CV and picture are of interest for a particular production, or an agent has strongly recommended you as being suitable for a specific part. Initially, you may see only the casting director, and then be called back later either to 'read' or 'screen test' for the director, or perform a suitable audition speech. An auditioner is just as anxious to cast the right actor or actress for the part as you are to get the job.

I talked to a group of actors and actresses at the Belgrade Theatre, Coventry, most of whom had left drama school within the past five years. They all felt it would be really helpful if they could have some advice from the auditioners themselves. Older actors also thought this would be useful. I asked some directors and casting directors to explain their side of the auditioning process and give some tips on the do's and don'ts of auditioning.

RUMU SEN-GUPTA – Producer for BBC Television; previously Joint Artistic Director of the Belgrade Theatre, Coventry:

'Some positive thoughts to remember when you audition:

1) What the director you're seeing wants most of all, is for someone to come in and walk away with the part. They don't want to agonise and be full of uncertainty. They are, therefore, hoping the moment you walk in, that you will be the right person for the part.
2) When you are called for an audition it is because something about you and your work has made you stand out from the rest. Directors receive increasingly large amounts of submissions from agents and individuals. The fact that you have been asked to audition is no small achievement on your part.
3) If you are asked to read or perform a piece, you have an ideal opportunity to show the director some of the qualities you have as an actor. It's not a performance that directors are looking for, it's the potential of what you have to offer.

4) All directors are human (although they may not appear to be)! Human beings enjoy positive contact with each other. The more you are able to contribute towards an enjoyable meeting, the more the audition will feel like it's going well, the more relaxed and confident you will become, and the more the likelihood exists of you landing the part.'

DON TAYLOR – theatre and television director and playwright – excerpts from his plays have been included in this book:

'Auditions and interviews are nerve-racking for actors because they are laying on the line not only their artistic selves but their livelihood. Rejection for an actor is always personal, in a way it is not for a playwright, because body and soul are being rejected, not something external that the artist has made . . . It is worth remembering that auditions are difficult for directors too. I often feel that the person most likely to get the job is the one that puts me at my ease. After all, if you enjoy meeting someone, have an interesting talk and some good serious work on the play, you are more likely to want to work with them, if only to renew an interesting acquaintance.

The director's difficulty, assuming he doesn't have a close acquaintance with the actor's work, is simply that he has to make a crucial judgement in a short time on insufficient evidence. If he gets it wrong, and casts the wrong person, his production will be doomed before rehearsal begins. All directors know this, and realise that there are times when they just have to play a hunch and hope that it works. To sum up an actor's potential – can he or she actually act, or is it merely a question of good reading technique, is the personality right for the part as far as the director conceives it, will the process of exploration go far enough and deep enough with this particular actor, or will it merely be a question of a polished surface and no heart? – in a brief meeting and perhaps a reading, is a daunting task. Very often a director might have half a dozen people, all of whom can act and will dig deep, all of whom are suitable for the part – not merely a question of looks, but of personality – and each one of whom will do it in a different way. Then the director has to consider making a working group with his other actors, and if that doesn't solve the problem, sleep on it, or in the final desperate analysis, simply toss a coin! I have never actually done that, physically, but I have once or twice done something mentally akin.'

KATIE REGAN – Casting and Producing, Katie Regan Ltd and Casting Support at the Hampstead Theatre, London. Katie has also worked as an actress in theatre, playing the lead in *How to Succeed in*

Business Without Really Trying, and on television – most recently in
Bad Girls and *Footballers' Wives*.

'Auditioning can naturally be a very nerve-wracking experience, whether
you are a new or an established actor. This said, any casting director is
delighted to find that perfect actor who fits the part, and directors equally
enjoy finding that "right person". Being the "right actor" can often depend
on the choice of piece you present during your audition.

The piece should reflect your own age and type. You should be famil-
iar with the character and have read the play. Be prepared, so that you
can expand upon the piece if asked to discuss it during an audition.

Before any audition, it is a good idea to understand the types of plays
the company is planning, to help you when choosing your piece. If you
are auditioning for a particular part, try to find a comparative piece and
if it is a general audition, it's good to have two contrasting speeches to
present, in order to give you a wider spectrum.

To give you some indication of the way casting works at the Hampstead
Theatre, they don't have a casting department as such, and don't as a
rule hold general auditions or send out casting breakdowns. Generally,
the creative team works with individual directors and often with freelance
casting directors to create lists of actors they are interested in meeting
for particular roles. They are always looking to increase the scope of such
lists by getting to see as many new productions as possible, from fringe
to West End, including readings, workshops, etc. You can write to let
them know when you are in a production, as they will always do their
best to get there.'

GILLIAN DIAMOND – Creative Consultant for Stanhope Productions;
previously Head of Casting with the Royal National Theatre and the
Royal Shakespeare Company. She also ran a course at the Drama
Centre, London, preparing third-year students for entry into the
profession.

'Read plays carefully and choose wisely to suit your strengths. Have a
variety of pieces and *keep changing them*, they quickly become stale and
therefore uninteresting. Be imaginative; wear clothes to assist your
character and chuck the trainers.

Always be natural and positive in interviews. Try and find out why
you are being seen and do some research on the playwright concerned.

If you know what the play is to be, read it thoroughly. Don't plead
lack of time, or lack of being informed as an excuse. Most people are
nice and wish you to succeed, so meet them with a positive attitude.

Never be grim. Try and be well informed and enthusiastic about the profession.

Remember that "many are called and few are chosen". All you can do is to come out knowing you have done your best – no regrets.'

GERRY O'HARA – has written and directed for films and television. He wrote the television adaptation of the mini-series *Operation Julie* and directed for *The Avengers, The Professionals* and other series. Earlier in his career he was Assistant Director to Laurence Olivier (*Richard III*), Carol Reed (*The Key* and *Our Man in Havana*), Otto Preminger (*Exodus* and *The Cardinal*), Vincente Minelli (*The Four Horsemen of the Apocalypse*), Tony Richardson (*Tom Jones*), Anatole Litvak (*Anastasia* and *The Journey*) and many others.

'Casting for films, and to some extent television, often involves an audition and a video test scene. The director usually tries to establish a rapport with the artiste. Certainly a relaxed informality is the best approach on both sides. The director may have a number of parts in mind; or may be storing up ideas for future productions.

The video "test" is usually a two or three page reading of a script that the artiste has not read in full and is often asked to tackle with as little as half-an-hour's notice. It is a tough proposition, even if it is prompted by necessity.

If the part is contemporary it is probably wisest to underplay, raising the temperature under the director's guidance. If you start by overplaying it is harder to quickly shrug off that approach and drop down as it were.

Casting a horror movie last year in Israel – American leads plus local supporting parts – it was interesting to see how heavily theatre-orientated players approached movie acting. Several of the established players had acted in European and American films and television and were completely at ease with the technique but those with years of experience in playing the theatres and one-night stands were steeped in a heavier style. And, of course, they were not playing in their own language. Here again the best advice was to underplay. The camera does the rest!'

RICHARD CALLANAN – Writer and director for films and television; Executive Producer, Children's Drama, BBC Television:

'Unlike the theatre, most auditions for television are for a single part so the producers have often a clear, if not blinkered, idea of what they are looking for. So the first job of the audition is to find out what they are looking for. This is not always easy. Established stars can ask for scripts in advance but most actors will have to get by with a garbled summary from their agent and perhaps a few pages of script when they arrive for interview.

The brutal reality of the process is that, again except for established stars, it is a buyer's market. Generous producers may have the good manners to disguise this power relationship but ignore it at your peril. This means that you must always be on time, or early, even if the producer is late or running an hour behind. You must be relaxed and cheerful even if the casting director has kept her head in the script from ten seconds after your entry. You must pretend it's a wonderful script even if you are gobsmacked that these wallies ever got the money to go ahead with the project.

So what do you do as you wait with a few paltry pages of script in your hands? If you are lucky you may also get a page summarising the story. Don't ignore this; it can give you valuable insights into your character, the style of the piece and, sometimes, the prejudice of the director. As you silently rehearse the piece in your mind don't get fixed on one interpretation. Think out three different ways to play the scene. You may not get a chance to try them but on your first read through you may feel an unreceptive frost coming across the table and you will be glad to suggest, "Of course it might be funnier to do it in Geordie – with a lisp."

I don't think it's a good idea to dress for the part. Producers usually like to think that they are adding something creative. So leave the Bank Manager's suit at home and keep the Tart's fishnet stockings for a party, However producers are not *that* creative so it's sensible to dress *towards* the part. Leave something to the imagination but don't make it an impossible challenge.

The interview will usually start with a little general chat, usually with your CV as the agenda – (so know what's on it)! Have a couple of "feelgood" stories to tell but be quick to notice when it's time to move on. If you have some questions on the production or the character, ask them now, not as you walk out the door.

Don't flirt. This advice applies equally to men and women! The myth of the Casting Couch must have some basis in history but I haven't come across it. Casting is one of the most crucial stages of production and the fear of getting it wrong is a perfect bromide for the libido. Anyway, casting is rarely done singly and flirting with one person is likely to get right up the nose of the other. I've seen it happen.

When reading the scene try to get it right rather than fast; it's an audition not a performance; an indication of potential, not achievement.

Make as much eye contact as possible. Eyes are all-important on television so you should also avoid any hairstyle that tends to hide them, even in a side-view.

When you have finished the scene don't be afraid to say, "Can I try that again?" Or "Can I try that standing-up?". This will usually open up a little conversation. Listen carefully to any suggestions made and be sure you understand them. Good directors will also be checking whether they can work well and communicate with you.

Finally, when the audition is clearly over, don't hang about. Don't start new and irrelevant conversations. The producers want you out of the room quickly so they can discuss you while you are fresh in their minds. Give them that chance or you could talk yourself out of a job!

Good Luckl!'

ALLAN FOENANDER – well-known film and television Casting Director for many years, with several thousand commercials and numerous feature films and TV films to his credit, including *Shirley Valentine* for Paramount – directed by Lewis Gilbert, *The Most Dangerous Man in the World* for BBC – directed by Gavin Millar, *Great Expectations* for Disney – directed by Kevin Connor, UK casting for *The Night of the Fox* – directed by Charles Jarrott, *Heidi* for Disney – directed by Michael Rhodes, *The Old Curiosity Shop* for Disney – directed by Kevin Connor and most recently the UK casting for *Buffalo Girls* for CBS – directed by Rod Hardy:

'Make sure your agent finds out what the project is about and do some research on it. Check you are free for the shoot dates.

Make sure you know where the casting session is taking place and continue to turn up on time even when experience will teach you waiting around is nearly always part of the deal.

You will find some casting directors or their assistants run cattle markets rather than casting sessions. Turn up if you like that sort of thing. At least you may meet friends!

You will be called for many casting sessions and, if the casting is being done to an accurate brief, you will meet some of your lifelong competition. Sometimes you will be chosen, most times you will not. Don't be discouraged. View every casting session as an opportunity – you are being called, you are meeting new directors and producers.

If it's a commercial, don't joke about the project! The director and casting director may share your humour, but remember the product client is bound to be in love with the big profit brand name and the advertising agency producer, if they value their job, will pretend to be.

If it's a film or television, brief yourself on the book or subject if you can. Never assume all directors and producers have imagination! If the casting director requests you to dress for the part, work on it. Also work at the reputation of being a reliable, willing and pleasant character who is never too grand, if available, to take any part.'

CAROLE BOYD – Actress; winner of BBC Radio Drama Company Carleton Hobbs Award 1996. Voice-overs and Audio books; plays 'Lynda Snell' in Radio 4's _The Archers_:

'If you want to work in radio, start by listening to it. I was lucky enough to grow up with it, so my ears and imagination kicked in instinctively from an early age. But it's by listening to radio, especially drama, that your imagination becomes engaged and creates your own unique sound picture for whatever you're hearing. It's the same for your listener, who, though seemingly invisible, actually has 'shared ownership' of that character, through _his_ or _her_ imagination – a big responsibility for an actor.

If you've had a brief and even a script for the part, try to "hear" the character's voice. Part of your toolkit should be a library of voices that you have developed from what you already know and from what you're constantly listening out for in real life. It's an ongoing study, because the truth of your character must be contained in the voice you give it. There are no visual aids in this medium – it's all in the voice, so work on your voice, take time to experiment, and practise sight reading – you'll need it.

There aren't many "auditions" as such, these days, for radio drama, but if you do get a call, apply all the wonderful advice already on offer in this book about punctuality, etc. Being a professional means knowing how to behave in a professional situation, even if other people don't. And if you get the job, be prepared to work hard and fast without too much chat – it's assumed that you know what you're doing.

Radio/voice work is exacting, demanding and often exciting, requiring both vocal and mental flexibility, but don't expect the same treatment you might get in television – no fancy fees, courtesy cars or big expense allowances. However, you will get the satisfaction of playing characters you'd never play visually, and you'll work with brilliantly talented people in a very warm and creative climate. Above all, you will develop immensely as an actor.'

ROY MARSDEN – Actor and director:

'I recommend this book to any actor, however experienced. The selection of audition pieces is extremely well chosen and the advice at the beginning is apposite and extremely useful. I have been an actor for half a century, having trained initially at Italia Conti and then at The Royal Academy of Dramatic Art. During this long period I have also directed many plays, ran theatre companies and lost an extraordinary amount of money. My brother runs a theatre company and art centre in Newcastle and my partner is a television producer. There is not much I haven't seen or experienced in the business, but when I look back it still doesn't add up to a can of beans. Every day is a new beginning and I still feel like an apprentice.

When I was a student, Peter Barkworth – certainly one of the greatest teachers of my generation – told me never to attend an audition if I didn't want the job. Sometimes an agent will encourage you to go and meet a director, casting people or a producer even if you aren't interested in the job. Bad move: you waste people's time. He also told me to prepare carefully for an audition, get there in plenty of time, and take a taxi. It's a special day, so treat yourself.

In this business rejection is the name of the game. It is inevitable that many of the jobs you go for you won't get, and at that time, for your own sense of well being, you rationalise your apparent failure by blaming the producer, the director, the play, or the conditions under which the audition took place. You can rave at your partner, kick the cat and despair in the pub, but deep down you know that no one is at fault, no one is to blame. Acting is not a competition, a race with winners and losers.

Don't get into the frame of mind of making yourself seem more important and knowledgeable by running down every show and performer you come across, and don't snigger with glee when some other poor sod of an actor, especially someone you know, gets bollocked by the critics, Your turn will come. Learn to be self-critical and trust in the views and advice of friends.

I have been for auditions which felt fantastic; the play was terrific, I was right for the part, I got on well with the director, we had a good meeting, everything was perfect. Afterwards I never heard another thing. Bastards! Other times it all goes wrong, you leave the audition in despair, and two days later your agent phones up and tells you they have offered you the job!

As a director I have held many auditions after which, at the end of the session and despite making copious notes, I couldn't distinguish one actor from another. Once it came down to remembering the actor I had seen four hours earlier because, for some curious reason, he'd been wearing odd socks. Be memorable. One fault common to many actors is a lack of internal energy. The dynamic, which is acting, comes from this energy. In an audition be alive, be strong, be vivid, be clear. Go in feeling great and come out feeling even better. Always travel with the thought that they were just as lucky to have met you, as you were to meet them. If you don't get the job, be pleased for the person who did. When I was a young actor I auditioned for the theatre director Joan Littlewood, and she asked me to "imagine you're a clown jumping in a safety net at a circus when you suddenly see a ship come steaming over the horizon". I sat and thought about it for a couple of minutes and then, with a sense of despair and failure, told her I couldn't think of anything. She laughed, took a drag of her fag and said, "Yes, you're right, it's a load of bollocks. Show me your mum ironing!"

Remember that, especially in television, producers and directors are trying to put together a group of actors who fit the story. Making the balance of the cast work requires more than just picking the most talented. The reason why one actor gets the job and another doesn't will have little to do with talent but rather the suitability of the actor for that role. In television they will look for someone who fits the character very closely, and so typecasting becomes more of a factor. They will have a strong idea of what they are looking for, and if you don't fit that pattern then there is little you can do. But if you impress them, there will always be another time, another play. People *do* remember.

It's a brave thing to be an actor; don't let anyone tell you differently. Through your career you'll experience lots of uplifting and thrilling events, but you'll also get kicked in the teeth. It's an industry hungry for new ways, new ideas and new talent. Be kind – not only to yourself, but to others.'

*At the back of this book there are an additional eight speeches, briefly outlined, for you to find and research for yourselves.

actresses'
audition speeches

Antigone – Set in Thebes/city of ancient Greece, young

ANTIGONE SOPHOCLES

TRANSLATED BY ROBERT FAGLES

Classical Greek play written in 441 BC and set in the royal house of Thebes. When the play opens, the sons of Oedipus – Eteocles and Polynices – have killed each other in battle and their uncle, Creon, is now King of Thebes. Creon has decreed that while Eteocles shall be buried with all due ceremony, Polynices must remain unburied because he fought against his own people. Anyone disobeying this order will be put to death. When **Antigone**, Polynices's sister, hears of the decree she determines to bury her brother, but is captured by the guards as she scatters dust over his body. She is brought before Creon, and in this speech defies her uncle, although she knows this means certain death.

Published in *Sophocles: Three Theban Plays*, by Penguin Classics

Antigone

Of course I did. It wasn't Zeus, not in the least,
who made this proclamation – not to me.
Nor did that Justice, dwelling with the gods
beneath the earth, ordain such laws for men.
Nor did I think your edict had such force
that you, a mere mortal, could override the gods,
the great unwritten, unshakable traditions.
They are alive, not just today or yesterday:
they live forever, from the first of time,
and no one knows when they first saw the light.

These laws – I was not about to break them,
not out of fear of some man's wounded pride,
and face the retribution of the gods.
Die I must, I've known it all my life –
how could I keep from knowing? – even without
your death-sentence ringing in my ears.
And if I am to die before my time
I consider that a gain. Who on earth,
alive in the midst of so much grief as I,
could fail to find his death a rich reward?
So for me at least, to meet this doom of yours
is precious little pain. But if I had allowed
my own mother's son to rot, an unburied corpse –
that would have been an agony! This is nothing.
And if my present actions strike you as foolish,
let's just say I've been accused of folly
by a fool.

Phebe – Warwickshire/rural, young

AS YOU LIKE IT WILLIAM SHAKESPEARE

Possibly first produced in 1599, this comedy is set mainly in the Forest of Arden, where Rosalind, disguised as a young shepherd, 'Ganymede', and her cousin Celia, seek refuge from the fury of the usurping Duke Frederick.

They encounter **Phebe**, a flirtatious young shepherdess, hotly pursued by the besotted Silvius. Rosalind 'chides' her for her unkindness to Silvius, telling her that as she has 'no beauty' she should accept 'his offer', and **Phebe** promptly falls in love with 'Ganymede'. In this speech she protests to Silvius that she really has no interest in 'Ganymede' but at the same time is unable to stop talking about him.

Act 3, Scene 5

Phebe

Think not I love him, though I ask for him;
'Tis but a peevish boy; yet he talks well.
But what care I for words? Yet words do well
When he that speaks them pleases those that hear.
It is a pretty youth – not very pretty;
But, sure, he's proud; and yet his pride becomes him.
He'll make a proper man. The best thing in him
Is his complexion; and faster than his tongue
Did make offence, his eye did heal it up.
He is not very tall; yet for his years he's tall;
His leg is but so-so; and yet 'tis well.
There was a pretty redness in his lip,
A little riper and more lusty red
Than that mix'd in his cheek; 'twas just the difference
Betwixt the constant red and mingled damask.
There be some women, Silvius, had they mark'd him
In parcels as I did, would have gone near
To fall in love with him; but, for my part,
I love him not, nor hate him not; and yet
I have more cause to hate him than to love him;
For what had he to do to chide at me?
He said mine eyes were black, and my hair black,
And, now I am rememb'red, scorn'd at me.
I marvel why I answer'd not again;
But that's all one: omittance is no quittance.
I'll write to him a very taunting letter,
And thou shalt bear it; wilt thou, Silvius?

Rita – Jewish, middle-aged

BAR MITZVAH BOY JACK ROSENTHAL

First transmitted on television in 1976 and set in Willesden, North London. **Rita** and her husband Victor have made elaborate preparations for their son Eliot's bar mitzvah and 117 guests have been invited to the dinner-dance at the Reuben Shulman Hall. Now Eliot has disappeared, and a thoroughly distraught **Rita** is lying on her bed, attended by her husband and future son-in-law, Harold.

Published by Penguin Books, London

Rita

Scene 55

(Rita stares into the middle distance. Extremely distraught, almost literally ill, she speaks with an ominous calmness – very slowly.)

RITA

Victor. At this moment . . . on their way . . . are 117 guests. At this moment. They're sitting on the train. In cars. Queuing for buses. All on their way. At half past six, Victor, 117 people from Bournemouth, from Manchester, Leeds and Glasgow, from Birmingham, everywhere, are going to turn up at the Reuben Shulman Hall expecting a dinner-dance. All dressed up. Your uncle Zalman. My cousin Freda. Your brother we don't talk about from Cardiff.

(VICTOR Ssssshhh. Don't upset yourself.)

RITA *(oblivious to him)* 117 people. 117 portions of chopped liver. 117 mushroom vol-au-vents. 117 chicken with croquette potatoes and helzel, French beans and cole slaw. 117 lokshen cuggles, a three-piece band – and no bar mitzvah boy. No bar mitzvah. No nothing.

(VICTOR It's no help upsetting yourself.)

RITA *(oblivious to him)* So, tell me, how do we cancel? How do we stop trains and cars and tell everyone to go home again? Do we stand on the M1 with a notice-board? Do we stand outside the Reuben Shulman Hall and tell them Eliot's gone for a walk and they've got no dinner? Ring Levy's and tell them we accidentally made a mistake – it was *next* year? What do we say? Do *we* go? Do *we* turn up? Do we ever show our face *again*? You're a clever man, you read the newspapers, you argue politics, tell me. I'd like to know.

(A helpless silence.
Rita's eyes start to fill up again.
Victor and Harold stare uselessly down at their shoes.)

(HAROLD Shall I ring the police again?)

(They ignore him. A silence.)

RITA 117 guests. All in their evenng suits. Long dresses. Sequin handbags.

Lizzie – American/Massachusetts, 33

BLOOD RELATIONS SHARON POLLOCK

First performed at Theatre 3, in Edmonton, Canada and in this country at The Canada House Cultural Centre, London in 1982. The play is set in 1902, with its 'dream thesis' set in 1892, at Fall River, Massachusetts. It explores the events leading up to the trial of thirty-three year old **Lizzie Borden**, accused and acquitted of killing her stepmother and father with an axe. In this 'dream thesis' scene, **Lizzie** confronts Mrs Borden and we see how she may well have killed her much-hated stepmother.

From *Plays By Women*, Volume Three, published by Methuen, London

Act 2

Lizzie

Did you know Papa killed my birds with the axe? He chopped off their heads. *(Mrs Borden is uneasy.)*. . . It's all right. At first I felt bad, but I feel better now. I feel much better now . . . I am a woman of decision, Mrs Borden. When I decide to do things, I do them, yes, I do. *(Smiles.)* How many times has Papa said – when Lizzie puts her mind to a thing, she does it – and I do . . . It's always me who puts the slug poison out because they eat all the flowers and you don't like that, do you? They're bad things, they must die. You see, not all life is precious, is it?
(Mrs Borden after a moment makes an attempt casually to gather together her things, to go upstairs. She does not want to be in the room with Lizzie.)
Where're you going?
    (MRS BORDEN Upstairs . . . *(An excuse.)* The spare room needs changing.)
(A knock at the back door . . . A second knock.)
LIZZIE Someone's at the door . . . *(A third knock.)* I'll get it.
(She exits to the kitchen, Mrs Borden waits, Lizzie returns. She's a bit out of breath. She carries a pile of clean clothes which she puts on the table. She looks at Mrs Borden.)
Did you want something?
    (MRS BORDEN Who was it? – the door?)

LIZZIE Oh yes. I forgot. I had to step out back for a moment and – it's a note. A message for you.

[MRS BORDEN Oh.]

LIZZIE Shall I open it?

[MRS BORDEN That's all right. *(She holds out her hand.)*]

LIZZIE Looks like Papa's handwriting . . . *(She passes over the note.)* Aren't you going to open it?

[MRS BORDEN I'll read it upstairs.]

LIZZIE Mrs Borden! . . . Would you mind . . . putting my clothes in my room? *(She gets some clothes from the table,* Mrs Borden *takes them, something she would never normally do. Before she can move away,* Lizzie *grabs her arm.)* Just a minute . . . I would like you to look into my eyes. What's the matter? Nothing's wrong. It's an experiment . . . Look right into them. Tell me . . . what do you see . . . can you see anything?

[MRS BORDEN . . . Myself.]

LIZZIE Yes. When a person dies, retained on her eye is the image of the last thing she saw. Isn't that interesting? *(Pause.)*

(Mrs Borden slowly starts upstairs. Lizzie *picks up the remaining clothes on the table. The hand hatchet is concealed beneath them. She follows* Mrs Borden *up the stairs.)*

Do you know something? If I were to kill someone, I would come up behind them very slowly and quietly. They would never even hear me, they would never turn around *(Mrs Borden stops on the stairs. She turns around to look at* Lizzie *who is behind her.)* They would be too frightened to turn around even if they heard me. They would be so afraid they'd see what they feared. *(Mrs Borden makes a move which might be an effort to go past* Lizzie *back down the stairs.* Lizzie *stops her.)* Careful. Don't fall. *(Mrs Borden turns and slowly continues up the stairs with* Lizzie *behind her.)* And then, I would strike them down. With them not turning around, they would retain no image of me on their eye. It would be better that way.

Barbie-Jean – Liverpool, 17

BREAK AWAY DAMEON GARNETT

First performed at the Finborough Theatre in March 2005 and set in Speke, Liverpool and Torqual, Devon in 2002.

When **Barbie-Jean**'s fun-loving Auntie Pauline wins a week's caravan holiday in Torquay, she invites **Barbie-Jean** and her friend, Stella, to join her. Boys figure high on their agenda and Stella and Auntie Pauline soon find themselves in demand. None of them are interested in **Barbie-Jean** and the two friends quarrel. To make matters worse, **Barbie-Jean**'s father and brother arrive and demand to join them in the caravan. **Barbie-Jean** is forced to spend most of her time alone on the beach, reading Oscar Wilde's *Lady Windermere's Fan* – a school book she just happened to bring along with her.

In this scene the family are back home again. **Barbie-Jean** has made up her mind to go to University and is sitting alone with her father reading a book of Wordsworth's poems. Her father picks up the Oscar Wilde and asks if she is 'still reading this play thing?'.

Published by Oberon, London

Barbie-Jean

Which one – *Lady Windermere's Fan*? No. I finished that ages ago . . . It's a bit sad . . . *(Speaking in a rush and excitedly.)* It's hard to explain. Basically, this girl, right, Lady Windermere, posh names of course, anyway, this woman turns up, Mrs Erlynne, anyway, Lady Windermere thinks she, Mrs Erlynne, is having sex with her husband, Lord Windermere – so she gets all hormonal and starts having an affair with this bloke, Lord Darlington, but she doesn't really; she just thinks about it. That's when it gets interesting – what she doesn't know, right, is that this woman, right, Mrs Erlynne, is actually her mother – Lady Windermere's mother. Not only that, but Mrs Erlynne – she's not even having it off with Lord Windermere. Of course, Mrs Erlynne knows the truth, I mean, about Lady Windermere, about Lady Windermere being her daughter. She knows that. So, anyway, right, Mrs Erlynne, right, sacrifices her own reputation to save her daughter's good name, Lady Windermere that is. But Lady Windermere still thinks Mrs Erlynne is really evil, until the end, right, when she realises that the only bitch is herself. So she forgives Mrs Erlynne, but without realising it's her mother, but if she knew it was her mother, if she knew how her mother really felt deep down inside, she might be happy.

  Pause.

Dad? . . . Are you listening?

  In fact he is dozing off. Barbie-Jean *goes back to reading her book.*
  Sound of the baby crying. Blackout.

Reeny – Liverpool, middle-aged

BREEZEBLOCK PARK WILLY RUSSELL

First presented at the Everyman Theatre, Liverpool in 1975 and later at the Whitehall Theatre, London. The action is divided between the respective houses of Syd and Betty and her sister **Reeny** and husband Ted, on a council housing estate over Christmas. A friendly and sometimes not so friendly rivalry exists between the two sisters.

Reeny is sitting at home watching television with Ted, her son John and brother Tommy and his wife Vera. Syd and Betty are due any moment. The night before, Betty's teenage daughter shocked the whole family with the announcement that she was pregnant. **Reeny**, secretly relishing the situation, says that poor Betty will be too ashamed to face them all.

Published by Samuel French, London

Act 2

Reeny

That poor, poor, woman.

(VERA Think she'll come round, Reeny?)

REENY . . . She won't be able to hold her head up any more. She must be dyin' with shame. *(Pause)* Mind you, it's her own fault. If she'd kept her eye on that girl it mightn't have happened. I mean, they might look grown up when they get to that age, but they don't know anything about the world. It's like him. *(Pointing to John)* He brought a girl home about six months ago, didn't you? He thought the sun shone out of her. But she didn't fool me – I could tell straightaway she was no good. A very murky girl, she was. It upset him like, didn't it, John?

(JOHN *(absently, still glued to the television)* Mmm.)

REENY But I had to explain to him. I mean it was my duty, Vera. I would never have forgiven meself if I'd kept quiet.

(VERA What was wrong with her, Reen?)

REENY What was right with her Vera? She had those eyes, y'know – very close together. His life would have been a misery if he'd carried on seein' her. Wouldn't it, John?

(JOHN *(repeating what he must have been told many times)* She wasn't the right girl for me. It was just infatuation.)

36

REENY As I say – he was upset for a bit – but our doctor's very good. He put him on Valium straightaway. They're marvellous things for settling you down. Show Aunty Vera your tablets, John. They do him a world of good. Don't they, John?

(John takes out a box of pills. Reeny takes them to show Vera, and retains them)

See, Vera, he's sensible, our John is. When me an' Ted saw how things were going with this girl, we said to him, didn't we, John, we said look, she'll do you no good, get rid of her, an' we'll see about gettin' you that little blue mini you've always fancied. It meant a bit of overtime but we didn't mind.

(VERA So John got the mini, did he, Reen?)

REENY I've told you Vera – that lad has got sense. He was brought up to think. Weren't you, John? . . .

See – we're a family here, Vera. We take an interest in our child. I mean, I'm not sayin' Betty's neglected that girl – but events speak for themselves. *(Pause)* God! How that woman must be sufferin' now. She's got my sympathy today.

(VERA She's got all our sympathy, Reen.)

REENY Tortured! Tortured with grief she'll be!

Mrs Pinchwife – Rural accent, young

THE COUNTRY WIFE WILLIAM WYCHERLEY

First performed in 1675 by the King's Company at the Theatre Royal Drury Lane. Jack Pinchwife, an old rake, has married a pretty young country girl and is determined to keep her away from the young 'gallants' about town. When he discovers that the notorious Master Horner has been paying his attentions to her and has even kissed her, he orders his young wife to sit down and write a letter to Master Horner telling him how much she hates and detests him. However, when he goes off to fetch wax and candle to seal it, **Mrs Pinchwife** determines to write a second letter and exchange it for the first.

Published by A & C Black, London

Act 4, scene 2

Mrs Pinchwife

'For Master Horner' – So, I am glad he has told me his name. Dear master Horner! But why should I send thee such a letter that will vex thee and make thee angry with me? – Well, I will not send it. – Ay, but then my husband will kill me – for I see plainly, he won't let me love Master Horner – but what care I for my husband? – I won't, so I won't send poor Master Horner such a letter – but then my husband – But oh, what if I writ at bottom, my husband made me write it? – Ay, but then my husband would see't – Can one have no shift? Ah, a London woman would have had a hundred presently. Stay – what if I should write a letter, and wrap it up like this, and write upon't too? Ay, but then my husband would see't – I don't know what to do – But yet i'vads I'll try, so I will – for I will not send this letter to poor Master Horner, come what will on't.

(She writes, and repeats what she hath writ)

'Dear Sweet Master Horner' – so – 'My husband would have me send you a base, rude, unmannerly letter – but I won't' – so – 'and would have me forbid you loving me – but I won't' – so – 'and would have me say to you, I hate you poor Master Horner – but I won't tell a lie for him' – there – 'for I'm sure if you and I were in the country at cards together' – so – 'I could not help treading on your toe under the table' – so – 'or rubbing knees with you, and staring in your face till you saw me' – very well – 'and then looking down and blushing for an hour together' – so – 'but I must make haste before my husband come; and now he has taught me to write letters, you shall have longer ones from me, who am, dear, dear, poor dear Master Horner, your most humble friend, and servant to command till death, Margery Pinchwife'. – Stay, I must give him a hint at bottom – so – now wrap it up just like t'other – so – now write 'For Master Horner'. – But, oh now, what shall I do with it? For here comes my husband.

shift	expedient
i'vads	in faith; rustic oath
hint at bottom	i.e., the postscript read by Horner at IV.iii.286–9

Madre – English/Set in Venice, late 40s

DAUGHTERS OF VENICE DON TAYLOR

First produced by the Chiswick Youth Theatre at the Waterman's Arts Centre in 1991 and then professionally by the Quercus Theatre Company at the Wilde Theatre in 1993, it is set in eighteenth century Venice. The 'Daughters' of the title are the orphans taken in and cared for by the Sisters of the Convent of the Pietà, famous for its choir and orchestra – the 'Coro'. **The Madre di Coro** is in charge of these young musicians. In this scene she persuades thirteen year old Perduta that she must leave her beloved Pietà and the Coro and go to live with her new found 'mother' – the wealthy Contessa di Montefalcone.

Published by Samuel French, London

Act 2

Madre

Now, my little copyist. You look most unhappy . . . I know how much you love it here, Perduta, life is full of things we love. You will learn as you get older that the story of our days is how, gradually, one by one, we lose them . . . You will have to go soon. In seven years . . . You will never get a better chance than the great joy of finding your own mother, who wants you, and will love you . . . you have been brought up in a convent, and know nothing of the world. She is a fine lady, intelligent, and for her sort, kind. She has a great need of you, and will love you very much: just as a mother should . . . Do not miss the chance, child. It comes only once in life, and if you miss it, it is gone for good. Venice is full of gondolas. Imagine if you were all alone on the island of tombs, and only one gondola could take you off. If you missed it, you would have to stay there alone, among the dead, for ever . . .
(Madre, without making a fuss of it, makes sure the door is fully closed and no-one is listening)
Let me tell you . . . something an old and very wise nun told me. A sad story . . . She was full of the love of Christ, even when she was a girl. She had always wanted to be a nun. But when she was fifteen, just as she was about to take her vows, she fell in love. She conducted a secret affair with her lover for two years. And was very, very happy . . . She found out that she was to have a child. And her lover deserted her . . . And her parents too: they threw her out in the street. She was in despair. But she had the child. All alone. It was a time of terrible anguish. And . . . She had it only a very short time. A few weeks. She couldn't manage on her own. She drowned her child, in the canal . . . And then she tried to drown herself. But she was saved. And brought here . . . The nuns saved her life, and she took her vows and became a sister of the order. But for the rest of her life . . . her whole life . . . She regretted that she had . . . thrown away the one person who would have loved her, the way children love their parents, and their parents love them. She would have had that. And she threw it away. Don't throw it away, Perduta. If you do, it is gone for ever . . . You do understand me, don't you. You have your life here at the moment, but it will pass, your friends will go and eventually you will have to go too. But where? To the nunnery yourself? Or the island of tombs?

Paulina – Set possibly in Chile. But could be any country that has a democratic government after a long period of dictatorship. 40

DEATH AND THE MAIDEN ARIEL DORFMAN

First performed in 1991 in London at the Royal Court Theatre and transferred the following year to the Duchess, the action takes place in present time in a country which is possibly Chile.

Paulina is married to Gerardo, a member of the Commission investigating crimes of the dictatorship. She is unable to erase from her mind the appalling tortures she suffered fifteen years ago and recognises the voice of their overnight guest, Roberto, as that of the doctor who supervised her torture. She binds and gags him while he sleeps and forces her husband, at gunpoint, to assist her.

On their own on the terrace, Gerardo asks her what she wants, and in this speech Paulina explains exactly what that is.

Published by Nick Hern Books, London

Act 2

Paulina

When I heard his voice last night, the first thought that rushed through my head, what I've been thinking all these years, when you would catch me with a look that you said was – abstract, fleeting, right? – you know what I was thinking of? Doing to them, systematically, minute by minute, instrument by instrument, what they did to me. Specifically to him, to the doctor . . . Because the others were so vulgar, so . . . but he would play Schubert, he would talk about science, he even quoted Nietzsche to me once.

(GERARDO Nietzsche.)

PAULINA I was horrified at myself. That I should have so much hatred inside – but it was the only way to fall asleep at night, the only way of going out with you to cocktail parties in spite of the fact that I couldn't help asking myself if one of the people there wasn't – perhaps not the exact same man, but one of those people might be . . . and so as not to go completely off my rocker and be able to deliver that Tavelli smile you say I'm going to have to continue to deliver – well, I would imagine pushing their head into a bucket of their own shit, or electricity, or when we would be making love and I could feel the possibility of an

DEATH AND THE MAIDEN

orgasm building, the very idea of currents going through my body would remind me and then – and then I had to fake it, fake it so you wouldn't know what I was thinking, so you wouldn't feel that it was your failure – oh Gerardo.

[GERARDO Oh, my love, my love.]

PAULINA So when I heard his voice, I thought the only thing I want is to have him raped, have someone fuck him, that's what I thought, that he should know just once what it is to . . . And as I can't rape – I thought that it was a sentence that you would have to carry out.

[GERARDO Don't go on, Paulina.]

PAULINA But then I told myself it would be difficult for you to collaborate in that scheme, after all you do need to have a certain degree of enthusiasm to –

[GERARDO Stop, Paulina.]

PAULINA So I asked myself if we couldn't use a broom. Yes, a broom, Gerardo, you know, a broomstick. But I began to realise that wasn't what I really wanted – something that physical. And you know what conclusion I came to, the only thing I really want?

Brief pause.

I want him to confess. I want him to sit in front of that cassette recorder and tell me what he did – not just to me, everything, to everybody – and then have him write it out in his own handwriting and sign it and I would keep a copy forever – with all the information, the names and data, all the details. That's what I want.

Linda – American/New York, middle-aged

DEATH OF A SALESMAN ARTHUR MILLER

First performed in England at the Phoenix Theatre, London in 1949, the action takes place in salesman Willy Loman's house and the places he visits in New York and Boston in the late 1940s. **Linda**, middle-aged and married to Willy, explains to her sons, Happy, who lives at home, and Biff, who has just returned after a year's absence, that they must make allowances for their father's erratic behaviour. The company he has been working with for over thirty years has taken his salary away, and for the last five weeks he has been working on commission only. Biff calls the company 'ungrateful baskets', but **Linda** points out that they are no more ungrateful than his own two sons.

Published by Penguin Books, London

Act 1

Linda

Are they any worse than his sons? When he brought them business, when he was young, they were glad to see him. But now his old friends, the old buyers that loved him so and always found some order to hand him in a pinch – they're all dead, retired. He used to be able to make six, seven calls a day in Boston. Now he takes his valises out of the car and puts them back and takes them out again and he's exhausted. Instead of walking he talks now. He drives seven hundred miles, and when he gets there no one knows him any more, no one welcomes him. And what goes through a man's mind, driving seven hundred miles home without having earned a cent? Why shouldn't he talk to himself? Why? When he has to go to Charley and borrow fifty dollars a week and pretend to me that it's his pay? How long can that go on? How long? You see what I'm sitting here and waiting for? And you tell me he has no character? The man who never worked a day but for your benefit? When does he get the medal for that? Is this his reward – to turn around at the age of sixty-three and find his sons, who he loved better than his life, one a philandering bum –

[HAPPY Mom!]

LINDA That's all you are, my baby! *(To Biff.)* And you! What happened to the love you had for him? You were such pals! How you used to talk to him on the phone every night! How lonely he was till he could come home to you!

Deidre – Irish/Aran, young
DEIDRE OF THE SORROWS J. M. SYNGE

Synge's last play, published posthumously and produced at the Abbey Theatre, Dublin in 1930, is a version of one of the great tragic legends of Ireland. **Deidre**, a young and beautiful girl, is destined to be the bride of an ageing King, Conchubor. She elopes with a younger man, Naisi, and after the 'magical' seven years, returns to her predicted death and the destruction of the city of Emain. In this scene she is crouching by Naisi's grave. Conchubor begs her to come back to him, but she tells him he is an old man and a fool. As she stands up, she sees the light from the burning city of Emain and at the end of her following speech, plunges Naisi's knife into her heart and sinks into the grave.

Published by Methuen, London

Act 3

Deidre

Deidre *stands up and sees the light from Emain*
Draw a little back with the squabbling of fools when I am broken up with misery. *She turns round.* I see the flames of Emain starting upward in the dark night; and because of me there will be weasels and wild cats crying on a lonely wall where there were queens and armies and red gold, the way there will be a story told of a ruined city and a raving king and a woman will be young for ever. *She looks round.* I see the trees naked and bare, and the moon shining. Little moon, little moon of Alban, it's lonesome you'll be this night, and to-morrow night, and long nights after, and you pacing the woods beyond Glen Laoi, looking every place for Deirdre and Naisi, the two lovers who slept so sweetly with each other . . . *(in a high and quiet tone)* I have put away sorrow like a shoe that is worn out and muddy, for it is I have had a life that will be envied by great companies. It was not by a low birth I made kings uneasy, and they sitting in the halls of Emain. It was not a low thing to be chosen by Conchubor, who was wise, and Naisi had no match for bravery. It is not a small thing to be rid of grey hairs, and the loosening of the teeth. *With a sort of triumph.* It was the choice of lives we had in the clear woods, and in the grave we're safe, surely . . . *(showing Naisi's knife)* I have a little key to unlock the prison of Naisi you'd shut upon his youth for ever. Keep back, Conchubor; for the High King who is your master has put his hands between us. *She half turns to the grave.* It was sorrows were foretold, but great joys were my share always; yet it is a cold place I must go to be with you, Naisi; and it's cold your arms will be this night that were warm about my neck so often . . . It's a pitiful thing to be talking out when your ears are shut to me. It's a pitiful thing, Conchubor, you have done this night in Emain; yet a thing will be a joy and triumph to the ends of life and time.
(She presses the knife into her heart and sinks into the grave.)

Mrs Dudgeon – American/New Hampshire, middle-aged/elderly

THE DEVIL'S DISCIPLE GEORGE BERNARD SHAW

First seen in New York in 1897 and produced in London at the Savoy Theatre in 1907. The opening scene is set in **Mrs Dudgeon**'s farmhouse kitchen in 1777. **Mrs Dudgeon** is an embittered elderly lady, who nevertheless has a reputation for piety and respectability among her neighbours. Her husband's brother, Uncle Peter, whom she loved years ago, has been hanged as a rebel and has left his daughter, Essie, in her care. She and Essie have been sitting up all night waiting for the return of Mr Dudgeon from 'the hanging'. Her youngest son, Christy, a fattish, stupid young man of twenty-two, arrives to break the news that his father is also dead.

Published in *Three Plays For Puritans*, by Penguin Books, London

Act 1

Mrs Dudgeon

MRS DUDGEON *(bursting into dry angry tears)*
Well, I do think this is hard on me – very hard on me. His brother, that was a disgrace to us all his life, gets hanged on the public gallows as a rebel; and your father, instead of staying at home where his duty was, with his own family, goes after him and dies, leaving everything on my shoulders. After sending this girl to me to take care of, too! *(She plucks her shawl vexedly over her ears)*. It's sinful, so it is: downright sinful.

(CHRISTY *(with a slow, bovine cheerfulness, after a pause)* I think it's going to be a fine morning, after all.)

MRS DUDGEON *(railing at him)* A fine morning! And your father newly dead! Where's your feelings, child?

(CHRISTY *(obstinately)* Well, I didnt mean any harm. I suppose a man may make a remark about the weather even if his father's dead.)

MRS DUDGEON *(bitterly)* A nice comfort my children are to me! One son a fool, and the other a lost sinner that's left his home to live with smugglers and gypsies and villains, the scum of the earth! . . . I want none of your sulks. Here: help me to set this table. *(They place the table in the middle of the room, with* Christy's *end towards the fireplace and* Mrs Dudgeon's *towards the sofa.* Christy *drops the table as soon as* *possible, and goes to the fire, leaving his mother to make the final adjust-ments of its position).* We shall have the minister back here with the lawyer and all the family to read the will before you have done toasting yourself. Go and wake that girl; and then light the stove in the shed: you can't have your breakfast here. And mind you wash yourself, and make yourself fit to receive the company. *(She punctuates these orders by going to the cupboard; unlocking it; and producing a decanter of wine, which has no doubt stood there untouched since the last state occasion in the family, and some glasses, which she sets on the table. Also two green ware plates, on one of which she puts a barnbrack with a knife beside it. On the other she shakes some biscuits out of a tin, putting back one or two, and counting the rest).* Now mind: there are ten biscuits there: let there be ten there when I come back after dressing myself. And keep your fingers off the raisins in that cake. And tell Essie the same. I suppose I can trust you to bring in the case of stuffed birds without breaking the glass? *(She replaces the tin in the cupboard, which she locks, pocketing the key carefully.)*

(CHRISTY *(lingering at the fire)* You'd better put the ink-stand instead, for the lawyer.*)*

MRS DUDGEON That's no answer to make to me, sir. Go and do as you're told. *(*Christy *turns sullenly to obey).* Stop: take down that shutter before you go, and let the daylight in: you can't expect me to do all the heavy work of the house with a great lout like you idling about.

Emma – American/New England, 20

DIFF'RENT EUGENE O'NEILL

First produced in New York in 1920, it is set in the parlour of the Crosby home, in a seaport village in New England, and covers a period between 1890 and 1920. **Emma Crosby**, aged 20, has always believed that her childhood sweetheart was 'diff'rent' from all the other men in the village. When she learns that he spent the night alone on board his ship with a naked South Sea Island girl, and is not so 'diff'rent' after all, she tells him that she cannot possibly marry him.

Published in *Collected Plays of Eugene O'Neill*, by Jonathan Cape, London

Act 1

Emma

Yes, I forgive
diff'rence – '
a pause – inte
don't. You nev
man would hav
from ever seeing
him understand.)
Caleb. Ever since
was – diff'rent. An
more and more. Ar
you. And now you'
more? I don't, Cal
something way down . . . Wait.
I don't want you to g ...ings. You 'n' me,
Caleb, we've been too ... ever get to be enemies. I like
you, Caleb, same's I alw ...ed. I want us to stay friends. I want you to
be like one of the family same's you've always been. There's no reason
you can't. I don't blame you – as a man – for what I wouldn't hold
against any other man. If I find I can't love you – that way – no more
or be your wife, it's just that I've decided – things being what they be
and me being what I am – I won't marry no man. I'll stay single. *(Forcing
a smile.)* I guess there's worse things than being an old maid . . .
(Shaking her head – slowly.) It ain't a question of time, Caleb. It's a
question of something being dead. And when a thing's died, time can't
make no diff'rence.

Zandile – Black South African, 8

HAVE YOU SEEN ZANDILE?

MARALIN VANRENEN at the Ma

First performed at the Edi
also as set in th
1987. It is set in
life. Zandile live
who dreams
turned u
and e
Tra

GCINA MHLOPHE,
ND THEMBI MTSHALI

ket Theatre, Johannesburg in 1986 and
nburgh Festival at the Traverse Theatre in
sixties and is based on Gcina Mhlophe's own
with her grandmother in Durban, a bright child
growing up to become a teacher – until her world is
ide down when she is kidnapped by her natural mother
pected to conform to the ways of life in the harsh, rural
skei homeland. In this scene **Zandile** is only eight years old. She
in her grandmother's garden speaking to the flowers as if they
are a class of children and she is their teacher. Note that **Zandile**
would be played by an adult actress, as the play spans approximately
ten years – from her childhood until her graduation.

Published by Heinemann, USA and Methuen, UK

Scene 4

Zandile

Ho ho ho ho! Good morning class! Good morning, Miss Zandile. And
what was all that noise I was hearing down the passage? Poor Miss Bongi
could hardly teach her Standard Twos. She teaches Nature Study, you
know, she's very clever. But do you know what happens to naughty
children? The white car will come for you and you won't even know it's
coming. It's going to be standing there and it will be too late to run.
Nobody can hear you scream because its engine makes such a loud
noise. They're going to take out your eyes and take you to a far away
place and nobody's going to see you ever again. *(She pauses as if she is
listening to something)* And what is that I'm hearing . . . is that the white
car? Ho ho ho ho! No, you are lucky this time. But I'm going to send
you straight to the principal's office and he is going to give you this *(she
demonstrates a hiding with her stick)* . . . Don't you know what day it is
today? It is the 21st of September 1966 and the inspector is coming here
today. You know the inspector does not understand our language *(she
starts giggling)* and we don't want to embarrass him. *(Puts her hand*

over her mouth and laughs) He cannot say our real names so we must all use white names in class today. Hands up those of you who don't have white names. We'll just have to give them to you. Wena you can be Violet. *(She points to different sections of the audience each time she mentions a different flower)* Petunia. Daisy. Sunflower and Innocentia . . . I don't know what that means . . . Do you know what name the inspector gave me in class today? Elsie. And I don't even look like an Elsie! Don't laugh! At least you are flowers. And do you know what he called Bongi? Moses! He couldn't even tell that she is a girl.

Now where was I? Good morning class. Good morning Miss Zandile. What can we do today? We could sing! This could be a singing class . . . if we get it right we can sing for the inspector, but if we get it wrong, then the white car will come for us.

The song is called Hamba kahle Vuyelwa *(She enunciates the title again)* Hamba – kahle – Vuyelwa

1, 2, 3, 4

(singing)	*Translation of song*
Hamba kahle Vuyelwa	Farewell, Vuyelwa
Usikhonzele emzini	Don't disgrace us to our in-laws
Kwandonga ziyaduma	God bless
Inkos' isikelele	God shower his blessings
Inkos' ithamsanqele	Farewell, Vuyelwa

Hamba Vuyelwa! *(The song breaks down)* . . . You don't want to sing Nina, he? You think I'm a fool opening my mouth like this ha ha ha nx! . . . *(Tearfully)* Hamba kahle Vuyelwa . . . *(she cannot take it anymore)* . . . You children don't want to sing. I'll teach you. *(Beats the ground with her stick)* He-e man, I'm not your friend, you are not my friends anymore, I'm going to call the white car for you . . .

Wena – you, hey you

Joan – French, young
HENRY VI PART I WILLIAM SHAKESPEARE

Historical play written between 1589 and 1591. The play opens with the death of Henry V and the accession of King Henry VI. In France, the English are being driven back towards the coast by the French, under **Joan of Arc**, portrayed here from the English point of view, as a woman of loose morals and a witch. In this scene, Rouen has been recaptured by the English and **Joan** waylays the Duke of Burgundy – the French nobleman who arranged peace between France and England in *Henry V* and then fought on the English side – and entices him back onto the side of the French.

Act 3

Joan

Look on thy country, look on fertile France,
And see the cities and the towns defac'd
By wasting ruin of the cruel foe;
As looks the mother on her lowly babe
When death doth close his tender dying eyes,
See, see the pining malady of France;
Behold the wounds, the most unnatural wounds,
Which thou thyself hast given her woeful breast.
O, turn thy edged sword another way;
Strike those that hurt, and hurt not those that help!
One drop of blood drawn from thy country's bosom
Should grieve thee more than streams of foreign gore.
Return thee therefore with a flood of tears,
And wash away thy country's stained spots . . .
Besides, all French and France exclaims on thee,
Doubting thy birth and lawful progeny.
Who join'st thou with but with a lordly nation
That will not trust thee but for profit's sake?
When Talbot hath set footing once in France,
And fashion'd thee that instrument of ill,
Who then but English Henry will be lord,
And thou be thrust out like a fugitive?
Call we to mind – and mark but this for proof:
Was not the Duke of Orleans thy foe?
And was he not in England prisoner?
But when they heard he was thine enemy
They set him free without his ransom paid,
In spite of Burgundy and all his friends.
See then, thou fight'st against thy countrymen,
And join'st with them will be thy slaughtermen.
Come, come, return; return, thou wandering lord;
Charles and the rest will take thee in their arms.

Margaret of Anjou – French, young

HENRY VI PART II WILLIAM SHAKESPEARE

Historical play written between 1589 and 1591. The marriage of Henry VI to **Margaret of Anjou** has worsened Henry's position in England. In Henry VI Part I, **Margaret** was a timid girl; now she is an enemy to York and Gloucester, despises her weak husband and is in love with the Lord of Suffolk, who brought her over from France to marry his King. In this scene **Margaret**, accompanied by Suffolk, has encountered four Petitioners, who are waiting to see the Lord Protector. She angrily tears up their supplications and sends them away, complaining to Suffolk about her situation and her disappointment in her husband.

Act 1, scene 3

Queen

My Lord of Suffolk, say, is this the guise,
Is this the fashions in the court of England?
Is this the government of Britain's isle,
And this the royalty of Albion's king?
What, shall King Henry be a pupil still,
Under the surly Gloucester's governance?
Am I a queen in title and in style,
And must be made a subject to a duke?
I tell thee, Pole, when in the city Tours
Thou ran'st a tilt in honour of my love
And stol'st away the ladies' hearts of France,
I thought King Henry had resembled thee
In courage, courtship, and proportion;
But all his mind is bent to holiness,
To number Ave-Maries on his beads;
His champions are the prophets and apostles;
His weapons, holy saws of sacred writ;
His study is his tilt-yard, and his loves
Are brazen images of canonized saints.
I would the college of the Cardinals
Would choose him Pope, and carry him to Rome,
And set the triple crown upon his head;
That were a state fit for his holiness.

Katharine – Spanish, middle-aged
HENRY VIII WILLIAM SHAKESPEARE

Historical play written in 1613. King Henry has met and fallen in love with Anne Bullen. He hopes to divorce **Katharine** – historically Catherine of Aragon – on the grounds that their marriage was not permissible as she was his brother's widow. **Katharine** is brought to court at Blackfriars and, in front of the Archbishop of Canterbury, the Cardinals and bishops, kneels before Henry and pleads her case.

Act 2, scene 4

(The Queen makes no answer, rises out of her chair, goes about the court, comes to the King, and kneels at his feet; then speaks.)

Katharine

Sir, I desire you do me right and justice,
And to bestow your pity on me; for
I am a most poor woman and a stranger,
Born out of your dominions, having here
No judge indifferent, nor no more assurance
Of equal friendship and proceeding. Alas, sir,
In what have I offended you? What cause
Hath my behaviour given to your displeasure
That thus you should proceed to put me off
And take your good grace from me?
Heaven witness,
I have been to you a true and humble wife,
At all times to your will conformable,
Ever in fear to kindle your dislike,
Yea, subject to your countenance – glad or sorry
As I saw it inclin'd. When was the hour
I ever contradicted your desire
Or made it not mine too? Or which of your friends
Have I not strove to love, although I knew
He were mine enemy? What friend of mine
That had to him deriv'd your anger did I
Continue in my liking? Nay, gave notice
He was from thence discharg'd? Sir, call to mind
That I have been your wife in this obedience
Upward of twenty years, and have been blest
With many children by you. If, in the course
And process of this time, you can report,
And prove it too against mine honour, aught,
My bond to wedlock or my love and duty,
Against your sacred person, in God's name,
Turn me away and let the foul'st contempt
Shut door upon me, and so give me up
To the sharp'st kind of justice.

Fanny – Lancashire, young/early 20s

HINDLE WAKES STANLEY HOUGHTON

First produced at the Aldwych Theatre, London in 1912, it is about Lancashire people in the small manufacturing town of Hindle. **Fanny Hawthorn** is a sturdy, determined young woman who works as a weaver at Daisy Bank Mill. She has spent the weekend with Alan, son of the owner of Daisy Bank, who is already engaged to Beatrice, the daughter of wealthy Sir Timothy Farrer. Alan's father has insisted that his son breaks off the engagement and does the 'right thing' by **Fanny**. She has other ideas and in this scene tells Alan that she doesn't love him, has no wish to marry him and that their weekend was only a bit of fun to her.

Published by Sidgwick & Jackson Ltd, London

Act 3

Fanny

Love you? Good heavens, of course not! Why on earth should I love you? You were just someone to have a bit of fun with. You were an amusement – a lark . . . You're a man, and I was your little fancy. Well, I'm a woman, and *you* were *my* little fancy. You wouldn't prevent a woman enjoying herself as well as a man, if she takes it into her head? . . . You're not good enough for me. The chap Fanny Hawthorn weds has got to be made of different stuff from you, my lad. *My* husband, if ever I have one, will be a man, not a fellow who'll throw over his girl at his father's bidding! Strikes me the sons of these rich manufacturers are all much alike. They seem a bit weak in the upper storey. It's their fathers' brass that's too much for them, happen! They don't know how to spend it properly. They're like chaps who can't carry their drink because they aren't used to it. The brass gets into their heads, like! . . . No. You're not a fool altogether. But there's summat lacking. You're not man enough for me. You're a nice lad, and I'm fond of you. But I couldn't ever marry you. We've had a right good time together, I'll never forget that. It *has* been a right good time, and no mistake! We've enjoyed ourselves proper! But all good times have to come to an end, and ours is over now. Come along, now, and bid me farewell . . . *(holding out her hand)* Good-bye, old lad . . . *(A slight pause.)* And now call them in again. Let's get it over.

Serafina Pekkala – Queen of the Lapland Witches

HIS DARK MATERIALS – PART TWO
NICHOLAS WRIGHT
ADAPTED FROM THE BOOKS OF PHILIP PULLMAN

First produced at the Royal National Theatre, London in December 2003 and adapted from Philip Pullman's novels into two full-length plays.

This is the second part of an epic tale that spreads itself across time and into strange worlds, old and new. At the centre is Lyra, described as a 'child of destiny', who unknown to herself has it in her power to bring about the annihilation of death and the triumph of the mysterious 'dust'. Accompanied by her friend, Will, she sets out to rescue her father, Lord Asriel, from the clutches of 'The Authority'.

The Lapland Witches have sworn to protect Lyra until her destiny can be fulfilled. They have been searching for her throughout the worlds and eventually **Serafina** finds her in 'Cittagazze' – with Will, lying sick on the ground beside her.

Published by Nick Hern Books, London

Serafina

It's hard for a witch to know what a short-lived girl like you might feel for a boy. We live so long, you see, for hundreds of years, never aging, never changing . . . and men are quite the opposite. They're like butter-flies, dead by nightfall. We no sooner fall in love with them, than they're gone. We bear their children, who are witches if they are girls . . . but mortals like their fathers if they are boys . . . and then we watch our sons growing strong and golden and handsome, knowing all the time that they'll die of old age, or on the battlefield, while we're still young, while we're still bearing son after son, each one of them just as doomed as the ones before. And finally our hearts are broken . . . I'd fallen to earth in the Fenland marshes, where Coram was fishing, and he hauled me into his boat, or I'd have drowned. He was twenty and I was pushing two hundred . . . Well, I lay a week in his cabin, with the light blocked out, while I was mending from my fall. But it was summer outside, and the light was calling. One afternoon we strolled across the fields. We picked fruits from the hedgerows . . . we sat, we talked, we watched the river . . . and I lifted a blackberry and pressed it against his lips. It was only then that I knew I loved him. Nine months later, I bore his child . . . He was a boy, and he died very young, in the great fever. It tore a piece out of my heart, and Coram was broken by it. I would have stayed and cared for him, but I had to fly back to the North to be Queen of my clan. I hoped that he would forget me, and find a human wife . . . It seems that our destinies were bound together after all, like yours and this boy's may be.

Nina – English, young

HIS HOUSE IN ORDER ARTHUR W. PINERO

Produced at the St James's Theatre, London in 1906 and set in a country mansion in the same period. Middle-aged member of parliament, Filmer Jesson, realising that his second wife, **Nina**, the young and pretty daughter of a clergyman, is incapable of keeping 'his house in order', invites his first wife's sister, Geraldine, to take over. Geraldine, together with her family, the Ridgeleys, makes life unbearable for **Nina**, by continually extolling the virtues of her predecessor, Annabel. In this scene, **Nina** has discovered letters written to the 'perfect' Annabel, by her lover, Major Maurewarde, and tells her friend and confidant, Mr Hilary Jesson, that she fully intends to make use of them.

Published by Samuel French, London

Act 3

Nina

You ask me whether I intend to make use of the letters. The question slipped out, but I'll answer it. Yes, I do intend to use them . . . What's to prevent me – or who? Or who? *(Gripping the letters through her bodice.)* Even if you snatched them away from me – tore them away from me – I *know*; I *know*. But I don't think you'd forget yourself to that extent . . . *(She sits upon the seat before the escritoire.)* While you are all out of the house – opening the park! – I shall shut myself up in my bedroom and copy the letters . . . Oh, yes, they shall enjoy their solemn parade . . . Afterwards – *(puckering her brows)* I shall put the copy into an envelope, with a note explaining how the originals came into my possession – . . . And see that Geraldine receives it directly she returns . . . I'm not hurting Filmer, much as he has hurt me – or the boy. Except for Maurewarde, the secret will be yours and mine – and the Ridgeleys'. Trust them to keep it. *(Walking to the fireplace.)* It's the Ridgeleys I'm aiming my blow at. *(Clenching her fists.)* The Ridgeleys! The Ridgeleys! . . . She shall crawl to me – Geraldine shall – as I've crawled to her; and you're right – she shall make them all crawl. Hilary – Mr. Jesson – often and often I've cried myself to sleep, after being tormented by Geraldine almost beyond endurance; cried half through the night. Now it's her turn, if she has a tear in her. *She* shall be meek and grovelling now, to *me* – consulting *my* wishes, *my* tastes, in everything; taking orders from me and carrying them out like a paid servant. I shan't be terrified any longer at her frown and her thin lips, but at a look from me she shall catch her breath – as I've done – and flush up, and lower those steely grey eyes of hers. And she won't be able to free herself from me. I've *got* her! I've got her, and she shan't leave me till I choose to dismiss her. *(Striking the back of the settee.)* Oh, she has tortured me – tortured me – she and her tribe; and from to-day –! You watch! You watch! *(She sinks down upon the settee weeping with anger.)*

Wife – 20s; Chinese optional

IN THE BAG WAN XIAOL

A VERSION BY RONAN O'DONNELL

This first-ever British production of a play from mainland China was premiered at the Traverse Theatre, Edinburgh in 2005.

Set in modern Beijing, it reflects the pressures of modern urban life and centres around two couples – known only as 'Man' and 'Woman', and 'Younger Brother' and **Wife**. **Wife** is in the early stages of pregnancy and cannot make up her mind whether to keep the baby or seek a termination. She is also a compulsive shopper and is fortunate that 'Younger Brother' is doing well enough in his business to support her extravagances.

In this scene **Wife** is waiting silently with her friend, 'Woman', for the lift in her apartment block. 'Woman' asks her what she is thinking about.

Published by Nick Hern Books, London

Wife

Those trousers, mmm . . . Everything in Esprit is big bucks. I was hesitating. Should I buy them or not, should I? They'd go against my cherry-perfect look, eh? Too 'career woman'. No, no, I've made up my mind. I'm buying them first thing tomorrow. Must have . . . Money makes you feel better. Tell me who do I hate? Nobody. The have-nots, they know how to hate – proper detest that doesn't stop like their boring grind doesn't stop. When I was small we had nothing. I remember the Spring Festival, it was live on TV. We didn't have a telly. I begged Mum to let me go to my uncle's to watch it. I was only little. But she kept saying no. 'Money's tight,' she said. No bus fare. I don't know how long I argued. My dad's pal joked, 'You'll get to see it tomorrow on the street corner when folks talk about it.' I don't remember if she relented. What I won't forget is shame in the dump, that feeling? The threadbare carpet was like a trophy to my mum. For visitors only. I don't want that for my kid . . . Now, he works so hard. Leaves dead early and comes back late. He's too tired to talk. He hits the sack right after he's bolted his tea. Last night I sat next to him to watch his face and he kicked me. He has bad dreams. It hurt so much I kicked him back. Then he punched me, so I shook him awake: 'Why did you punch me?' He was gasping, 'I was fighting a bogey, ugly monster. Shouting on it to "fly, fly away", and it leapt on top of my computer. When you were shaking me it was like it had flown back onto me and wasn't letting go!' He was so funny. I laughed till tears were running down my face. How can a baby like that be a dad? You know what he said next? I really love him for it. He was lying there in his sweat, staring at the ceiling. I could feel his heart beating beneath my hand . . . 'I earn money to take care of you – the want can never hurt you again. And if . . . if anything happens to me you'll be well sorted.'

Why was he dreaming of a monster? Most likely cos I put him under too much pressure . . . Why do I only think of shops? I'm obsessed. I'm in a shop and I feel like I belong. I'm totally at home. People don't realise comfortable is such an intense thrill. The till and card swipe is so beautiful. Money can't buy you happiness but without it you feel there is no chance. I don't know – I must be bored. I must be.

Sasha – translated from Russian, 20

IVANOV ANTON CHEKHOV

TRANSLATED BY ELISAVETA FEN

First produced at the Alexandrinsky Theatre in St Petersburg in 1887 and set in one of the provinces in central Russia. **Sasha**, aged twenty, daughter of the Chairman of the County Council, is about to marry Ivanov, a man discontented with life and almost twice her age. On the wedding morning, he tells her that he cannot go through with the marriage and ruin her life, as he feels he ruined the life of his previous wife, Anna. Lvov, a young doctor who has always hated Ivanov and blames him for Anna's death, insults Ivanov, calling him a cad in front of his guests. **Sasha** turns on the doctor, accusing him of spreading malicious rumours and interfering with their lives.

Published by Penguin Books, London

Act 4

Sasha

(To Lvov*)*

What did you do it for? What did you insult him for? My friends, please make him tell me what he did it for! . . . Well, what do you want to say? That you're an honest man? All the world knows that! I'd rather you told me whether you understand yourself, or whether you don't. You just came in here now and hurled a shocking insult at him which nearly killed me – you did that as an honest man; before that you'd been pursuing him like a shadow and interfering with his life, and, of course, you did that too in the certainty that you were fulfilling your duty, that you were an honest man. You meddled with his private life, you slandered and ran him down whenever you could; you bombarded me and all my friends with anonymous letters – and all the time you were doing it you thought of yourself as an honest man. Yes, Doctor, you thought it was honest not even to spare his sick wife, to keep on worrying her with your suspicions. And whatever you may do in the future – acts of violence, or cruelty, or meanness – you'll still think yourself an extraordinarily honest and high-minded person! . . . So just think that over: do you understand yourself, or don't you? Stupid, heartless creatures! *(Takes* Ivanov's *hand.)* Let us go from here, Nikolai! Father, come! . . .

(IVANOV Go? Where to? Just wait a moment, I'll put an end to all this! I can feel youth waking up in me – the old Ivanov speaks again! *(Takes out a revolver.)*)

SASHA *(shrieks)*. I know what he's going to do! Nikolai, for God's sake! . . . *(shrieks)* Nikolai, for God's sake! Stop him!

(IVANOV Leave me alone! *(Runs aside and shoots himself.)*)

Rena – 20s, Black American
JITNEY AUGUST WILSON

First produced in Great Britain at the Royal National Theatre in 2001. It is set in a Jitney Station in Pittsburgh, Pennsylvania and depicts a firm of cab drivers who serve the black neighbourhoods.

The station is run by Becker, a well-respected man in his 60s, whose son has just come out of prison. His drivers are Turnbo, who always has his nose in other people's business; Fielding who has an alcohol problem; Doub, a Vietnam veteran; and Youngblood in his early 20s. Youngblood and his girlfriend, **Rena**, are struggling to make a life for themselves and their young son. Youngblood is hardly ever at home these days and rumour has it he is running around with **Rena**'s sister, 'Peaches'.

In this scene **Rena** has called in at the Jitney Station. Youngblood is out on a trip. Turnbo tells her that Youngblood is not good enough for her; she deserves someone better. When Youngblood comes in, she confronts him. What has happened to the food money? She has just got back from work to find that 80 dollars has gone.

Published by Nick Hern Books, London

Rena

Darnell, I want to see you . . . Darnell, I don't understand. I try so hard.
I'm doing everything I can to try and make this work . . . I'm working
my little job down there at the restaurant . . . going to school . . . trying
to take care of Jesse . . . trying to take care of your needs . . . trying to
keep the house together . . . trying to make everything better. Now, I
come home from work I got to go to the store. I go upstairs and look in
the drawer and the food money is gone. Now you explain that to me.
There was eighty dollars in the drawer that ain't in there now . . . You
know I don't touch the grocery money. Whatever happens we got to eat.
If I need clothes . . . I do without. My little personal stuff . . . I do
without. If I ain't got no electricity . . . I do without . . . but I don't never
touch the grocery money. Cause I'm not gonna be that irresponsible to
my child. Cause he depend on me. I'm not going to be that irresponsible to my family. I ain't gonna be like that. Jesse gonna have a chance
at life. He ain't going to school hungry cause I spent the grocery money
on some nail polish or some Afro Sheen. He ain't gonna be laying up
in the bed hungry and unable to sleep cause his daddy took the grocery
money to pay a debt . . . It ain't all about the money, Darnell. I'm
talking about the way you been doing. You ain't never home no more
. . . You be out half the night. I wake up and you ain't there . . . I just
want you to know I ain't no fool, Darnell. I know you been running
around with Peaches and her crowd all hours of the night. Doing
whatever you be doing. I may not know everything but I know
something's going on. I know you all doing something . . . She's my
sister, Darnell. Don't you think I can tell she's trying to hide something
from me . . . Ain't no need in you bothering to come home cause I just
might not be there when you get there.
Rena exits.

Jitney   a small bus carrying passengers for a low fare.

Snake – Australian, 18

THE KID MICHAEL GOW

First performed by the Nimrod Theatre Company, which was founded in 1970. It is set in a blazing Sydney summer in the present. **Snake** is eighteen and has two brothers; Aspro, who is very sick, and Dean who is very, very healthy. They are all on a quest, heading for Valhalla in a red mini – which they shouldn't be driving. On the way they are joined by Donald, an opera fanatic fresh out of school. They are all forced to take up residence in the largest block of flats in the Southern Hemisphere. **Snake** is telling Donald how much she hates this trip.

Published by Currency Press, Australia

Scene 3

Snake

Honestly. I hate this trip. It's always chaos. Always a fight. By the time we get to Auntie Eileen's no one's talking to anyone. I have to do everything. Get the boys ready. Stock up on drinks and Marlboro and chips. Hate it. Won't it be great when we get the money? We'll be happy. We might take over a service station. Dean can fool around with his engines. I'll cook snacks and Pro can man the pumps. I'll have to help him with the change. I'll look back on all this and laugh. Hate it. All the people we end up taking along. Dean always collects someone.

(DONALD I see.)

SNAKE You must have been the first one ever to turn him down. He was that upset. He was driving like a maniac. He just drove over the median strip and back we came. Little turd. Know why he got chucked out of school? Mrs Tucker – guess what Dean called her – was wrapped in him. She used to beat shit out of him, for any reason, no reason, just so she could grab hold of him and whack his bum. One day he'd had enough and he told her to go and see one of the Abo stockmen and he'd fix her up. Poor woman grabbed all the rulers in the room and laid into Dean. He stood up, gave her a right hook and she went down like a ton of bricks. We all stood on the desks and cheered. I reckon Dean would win wars single-handed. The enemy would come to him on bended knees. People will do anything just to get a wink or a smile that says he likes you. Little turd. Foul temper. Lazy. But who cares when it's Dean?

Ellida – Set in Norway, young/30s

THE LADY FROM THE SEA HENRIK IBSEN

TRANSLATED BY PETER WATTS

First produced at the Kristiania Theatre, Oslo in 1889, it is set in a small town on a fiord in northern Norway. **Ellida**, the second wife of middle-aged Dr Wangel, has always had an affinity with the sea. She loves her husband, but is haunted by the memory of the sailor she was once engaged to, who stabbed his captain to death and escaped to the north. Now, ten years later he has returned, and although she is frightened of him, she finds herself drawn towards him by a strange magnetism. He reminds her of the vows they once made, and insists that she belongs only to him. He will return the next day and take her away with him. In this scene, **Ellida** tells her husband that she must be free to choose her own destiny – it is her only salvation.

Published in *A Doll's House and Other Plays*, by Penguin Classics

Act 5

Ellida

No one can stop me from choosing – not you, nor anyone else. You can forbid me to go with him, or follow him, if that is what I choose. You can keep me here by force, against my will. Yes, you can do that. But you cannot stop me choosing – in my innermost heart . . . choosing him instead of you – if that has to be my choice.

(WANGEL No, you are right – I can't stop that.)

ELLIDA And I have nothing whatever to hinder me; here at home there's nothing in the world to hold me. Oh, Wangel, I have no roots whatever in your house. The children don't belong to me – not in their hearts, I mean – they never have done. When I go away – if I do go – whether it's with him tonight, or out to Skjoldvik tomorrow – I'll not have a single key to hand over, no orders to give about anything at all. I'm so utterly without roots in your house. Even from the very beginning I've been like a complete outsider here.

(WANGEL But you wanted it to be like that.)

ELLIDA . . . I simply let everything stay just as I found it the day I came. It was you who wanted it that way, and no one else.

(WANGEL I thought that would be the best for you.)

ELLIDA . . . and now we have to pay for it – it's taking its revenge. Because now there's nothing here to hold me, nothing to help me, nothing to give me strength. I have no ties with what should have been our most precious possession.

(WANGEL I do realise that, Ellida. That's why, from tomorrow, you shall have your freedom again and be able to live your own life.)

ELLIDA You call it my own life! No, my own life – my true life – went astray when I joined it to yours. *(Wringing her hands in pain and agitation)* And now tonight – in half an hour – the man whom I failed will be here. The man to whom I ought to have been as completely faithful as he has been to me. And now he's coming to offer me my last and only chance to live my own true life – the life that frightens yet fascinates me – and that I cannot renounce, not of my own free will.

Cattrin – Welsh, 29

THE LIGHT OF HEART EMLYN WILLIAMS

First produced at the Apollo Theatre, London in 1940, the action takes place in furnished lodgings at the top of a house in Long Acre, London WC2.

Cattrin, a young woman with a crippled foot, has spent most of her life looking after her father, Maddoc Thomas – a fine actor in his day, whose career has been ruined by his fondness for drink. Now he has the chance to work again and Cattrin, feeling her obligation to her father is now over, plans to marry and go to live in America. In this scene, Mrs Lothian, a rich woman who has put up the money for Maddoc's comeback, tells Cattrin that her father needs her more than ever and begs her not to leave him. Cattrin replies that she has her own life to lead now.

Published in *The Collected Plays of Emlyn Williams*, by Heinemann, London

Act 3, scene 1

Cattrin

(Swinging on her, in a sudden outburst)
His life – what about *my* life? . . . *(Calmer.)* I loathe scenes . . . *(After an effort.)* I've never indulged in self-pity, Mrs Lothian, but I've got to do it now. *(Choosing her words.)* I could have made a career in music, I let it go; I like new people, and Robert's the first I've met for eight years; I loathe dirt and disorder, and for as long as I can remember I've rubbed shoulders with both; I have a great liking for – grass, and trees, and – and the only time I've been to the country was to see a friend married. I'm fond of children . . . For eight years, I've been a prisoner in this room, and I've served my sentence as faithfully as I knew how. I've cheered him up when he was depressed, lied to him if it made him happier, pretended he couldn't have been sick the night before because the room was as clean as a new pin – and while that's been going on, time's been going on too. Twenty-nine isn't old, but it's quite a time to catch up; there's a chance to catch up now. Before God and my conscience, that I've searched into through whole anxious nights, I have the right to take that chance. And nothing in the world is going to stop me. That's all . . . how can you talk about a wreck? *(Sitting on the sofa back, speaking with the emphasis of self-justification.)* You see him as he was that first evening here, don't you? A year ago? In that year I've seen a miracle working on my father. He hasn't just been excited by the idea of success; he's been sitting at that table – striding about this room – with a light in his eye. And that light showed, beyond a doubt, that he's doing the supreme work he was born to do, and that only he can do. If you'd been here this morning and heard him talk about it, quite quietly . . . You told him he'd been dead and buried for eight years, do you remember? Well, tonight he's going to live again. The typist can leave, because the business is on its feet at last.

Sheila – 50s

LOSING LOUIS SIMON DA COSTA

This comedy was first performed at the Hampstead Theatre in January 2005 and then transferred to the Whitehall Theatre, London. The action takes place in one large bedroom with scenes alternating between past and present time.

In this scene, Jewish and non-Jewish family members, who haven't seen each other for years, are brought together for Louis' funeral. The ceremony has been a disaster, with the hearse breaking down in the pouring rain and the coffin, covered with a black bin liner, brought to the cemetery in a hatchback. Back at the house, everyone is wet and dishevelled, tempers are frayed and insults are exchanged between Louis' two sons, Tony and Reggie and their wives **Sheila** and Elizabeth. Long-buried family secrets are revealed, tears are shed and **Sheila** suggests that perhaps they might tell a few jokes to liven the atmosphere. Louis loved a laugh.

Published by Methuen Publishing, London

Sheila

This is a really great one. You'll love this. There's this dear old lady and she's really upset because her husband Albert has just passed away. She goes to the undertaker's to have one last look at her dearly departed husband, but the moment she sees him, she starts crying. One of the undertakers rushes up to give her some comfort. Through her tears she explains that she is upset because her dear Albert was wearing a black suit, and it was his dying wish to be buried in a blue suit . . . the undertaker apologises and explains that traditionally, they always put the bodies in a black suit, but he'd see what he could arrange . . . Ssh. Ssh. The next day she returns to the undertaker's to have one last moment with Albert before his funeral the following day. When the undertaker pulls back the curtain, she manages to smile through her tears as Albert is decked out beautifully in a smart blue suit. She says to the undertaker 'Wonderful, wonderful, but where did you get that beautiful blue suit?' The undertaker replied, 'Well, yesterday afternoon, after you left, a man about your husband's size was brought in and he was wearing a blue suit. His wife explained that she was very upset as he had always wanted to be buried in a black suit.' The old lady smiled at the undertaker. He continued, 'After that, it was simply a matter of swapping the heads.' . . .

[Reggie picks up the cake and exits.]

. . . What did I say? Reggie told one about funerals. Reggie! *(She exits.)* Reggie. Sorry. I didn't mean anything by it.

Lorna – late 20s

MAMMALS AMELIA BULLMORE

First produced at the Bush Theatre in April 2005. The action throughout takes place in the kitchen.

Jane and Kev are a happily married couple with two young
children. They've agreed never to keep secrets from one another,
but when Kev comes home early from a business trip and tells Jane
he has fallen in love with a girl at work, he sets off a chain-reaction
of confessions leading to disastrous consequences.

In the midst of all the explanations and recriminations his best
friend Phil arrives unexpectedly with his girlfriend, **Lorna** – a tall,
elegant, outspoken young woman who runs a successful business
designing expensive handbags. She announces that she and Phil
have just had 'a huge row' in the car.

In this scene **Lorna** is on her own in the kitchen with Jane. Phil
has already told her about Kev's confession and now she wants to
hear Jane's side of the story. Jane reluctantly tells her as much as
she knows. Then to her surprise, **Lorna** reveals that she has never
really loved Phil.

Published by Methuen Publishing, London

Lorna

I don't love Phil . . . the man I'm waiting for picked me up and put me down and picked me up and put me down for three years till I didn't know what my name was. I lived on apples for a year. I had to sleep with a pillow between my knees if I lay on my side because my own bones kept me awake. We finished five years ago. I don't know where he is. Amsterdam's the last I heard. I look for him everywhere I go. I've scanned every station platform, every bus stop, every cinema queue, every garage forecourt – anywhere peopled – for five years. What I've been *doing* is making bags, setting up the business looking like I'm living – but what I've really been doing is waiting for him. And if he comes for me, I'll go. Not for the pain. I've no interest in pain. What I'm after is the end of the story . . . What I feel for Phil – most people, if they felt it, would stand up in court and swear it was love! It's what's come to be known as love. Rubbing along, having a laugh, having enough of the kind of sex you like, liking them enough to put up with the terrible things they do because they're not you. That's what we call love. And all the millions of people who feel that, thank their lucky stars they're in the love room and not outside it, cold and lonely. But the love room's a con. The love room is actually just a holding space. But the very very lucky few, casually leaning on a wall in the love room, occasionally, accidentally open a hidden door and fall through to the *real* love room. Which is smaller and emptier and totally beautiful. I've been there. But not with Phil.

Hannah – American, 30–40

THE NIGHT OF THE IGUANA
TENNESSEE WILLIAMS

First presented at the Royale Theater in New York in 1961, the play takes place in the summer of 1940 at the Costa Verde, a rustic and very Bohemian hotel in Puerto Barrio, Mexico. **Hannah**, a good-looking spinster, aged somewhere between thirty and forty, arrives at the hotel looking for rooms for herself and her ancient poet grandfather, Nonno. She is a painter and a 'quick sketch artist', paying her way by selling water colours and sketching hotel guests. In this scene she talks to Shannon, a defrocked priest turned travel guide, who is 'cracking up' and has to be restrained from 'swimming out to China'.

Published by Penguin Books, London

Act 3

Hannah

You see, in my profession I have to look hard and close at human faces in order to catch something in them before they get restless and call out, 'Waiter, the check, we're leaving.' Of course sometimes, a few times, I just see blobs of wet dough that pass for human faces, with bits of jelly for eyes. Then I cue in Nonno to give a recitation, because I can't draw such faces. But those aren't the usual faces, I don't think they're even real. Most times I *do* see something, and I can catch it – I *can*, like I caught something in your face when I sketched you this afternoon with your eyes open. Are you still listening to me? *(He crouches beside her chair, looking up at her intently.)* In Shanghai, Shannon, there is a place that's called the House for the Dying – the old and penniless dying, whose younger, penniless living children and grandchildren take them there for them to get through with their dying on pallets, on straw mats. The first time I went there it shocked me, I ran away from it. But I came back later and I saw that their children and grandchildren and the custodians of the place had put little comforts beside their death-pallets, little flowers and opium candies and religious emblems. That made me able to stay to draw their dying faces. Sometimes only their eyes were still alive, but, Mr. Shannon, those eyes of the penniless dying with those last little comforts beside them, I tell you, Mr. Shannon, those eyes looked up with their last dim life left in them as clear as the stars in the Southern Cross, Mr. Shannon. And now . . . now I am going to say something to you that will sound like something that only the spinster granddaughter of a minor romantic poet is likely to say . . . Nothing I've ever seen has seemed as beautiful to me, not even the view from this verandah between the sky and the still-water beach, and lately . . . lately my grandfather's eyes have looked up at me like that . . .

Eileen – 30s, Oldham, Lancashire
NOT WITH A BANG MIKE HARDING

A comedy first performed at the Coliseum Theatre, Oldham in 1983. It is described as 'a wry look at the nuclear disarmament issue'.

Territorial Army pals, Nobby, Tommy and Ken think it's all a big joke when their wives join the Women's Peace Movement, but when the women are seen on television demonstrating outside the American air base the men become the laughing stock of their battalion. The final straw comes when the women try to make their husbands give up the Army by going on a sexual strike with their slogan, 'No Nooky against Nukes'.

In this scene, **Eileen** and Norma come into the front room carrying shopping bags. They flop down on the settee. Bella comes in with the tea. **Eileen** confesses that the sexual strike is beginning to get her down. It is now three months since they started their campaign.

Published by Samuel French, London

Eileen

Well I don't know, it's getting me down a bit now this. I mean it's been three months. I never thought we'd last out. I mean I was never very physical, you know, didn't even like Postman's Knock when I was a kid or going on the hobby-horse in the playground, but I think I'm starting to feel a bit frustrated now. You know this morning I was reaching for something on the top shelf in the kitchen and as I was leaning up against the washing-machine it started going to spin dry and all the vibrations went through me and it got me – *(she stops)*. . . . Well I don't know how to say really. I mean, I thought, ooh that's nice and I just sort of stayed there and kept it on fast hot wash and spin . . . Well, then there was a knock at the door and I knew it was the Co-op dairy for his money, and well me legs were all shakin' and that and you know I told you about him, him with the red 'air and the moustache, the really 'andsome one that looks like Jess Conrad, you know the one that keeps smiling at me – he's just got divorced you know by the way. Well, I went to the door and I felt like I was in a dream. I was all twitchy and, and well, hot and shaky and I opened the door and, ooh I feel stupid . . . Well it was the other one, his little bandy mate with the squint and no teeth, so I just burst out crying and said 'No yoghurt on Saturday' and ran back in.

Alice – 35, Lancashire

ON THE SHORE OF THE WIDE WORLD
SIMON STEPHENS

First presented at the Royal Exchange Theatre, Manchester in 2005. It is set in Stockport in 2004 and is a play about family love, loss and eventual recovery.

Peter Holmes and his wife, **Alice**, have been married for almost 20 years and have two sons, Alex and Christopher. A happy, easy-going family – until Christopher is killed in a car accident and their lives seem changed irrevocably. Peter has taken over his father's business restoring old buildings, and is becoming more and more engrossed in his work. He and **Alice** have little time for each other now.

John Robinson, the driver of the car that killed their son, calls to see **Alice**. He needs to talk about what happened At first she refuses to have anything to do with him, but he insists on leaving his card. Eventually she telephones him and they meet up in a café in the centre of Stockport. They talk about everything but the accident, and as John gets up to leave, **Alice** says she would like to see him again.

The next evening **Alice** is in John's flat. They are drinking wine and smoking cigarettes. As he refills her glass, she starts to tell him how she and Peter first met.

Published by Methuen Drama, London

Alice

He used to come into the office. That was where the account for his yard was held. . . .

(John refills their wine glasses.)

. . . So he'd come in every Friday. Which is when I'd be working, after I finished college. I just ended up chatting to him. He seemed to always want to come and make his payments to me. That might just be my imagination, by the way. And this was what, twenty years ago, and he is a heart-stoppingly handsome man. He's tall and he's lean and he has these shoulders. And every week he's coming in and over the course of a few months the conversation starts getting more and more flirty. And I love it. I do. It's like he's flirting without making me uncomfortable or unhappy or . . . So I ask him out . . . Yeah. I do. And I think he is a little taken aback. I mean, I'm just a sixth-former with a weekend job. But he does say yes. And he takes me to the cinema. He buys us the tickets. I buy us some fish and chips for our tea on the way home . . . I kiss him for the first time on our first date. He has the softest lips which surprises me. For a man with these – he works with his hands. And the skin on his hands is hard. But his lips are like – Two nights later I sleep with him and for me it's the first time. You know? . . . I'm seventeen. We have sex four times and then on the fifth time . . . I'm pregnant . . . I don't answer his calls for three days. You know, I don't know what to do. I go round and see him four days later and by this stage he's quite surprised to see me. When I tell him, he's sitting on his bed, this little single bed, with this duvet, and what he's doing is, he's crying. I dry his eyes for him. We talk and we decide the sensible thing to do, because of my A-levels, and because of his work, is for me to have an abortion. And I leave. And two weeks later he comes round and tells me not to. That he's been thinking about it. That he thinks that what he wants to do instead of me having an abortion is, he wants to ask me to marry him. Basically. *(Pause.)* And so he does. And I say yes. And we do. And I leave college. And. I was always going to go back but then Christopher. *(Pause.)* I've not smoked in six years . . . If he finds out, he'll kill me . . .

Beat. She stubs her cigarette out.

. . . He goes to the grave, to Christopher's. All the ime . . . He doesn't think that I know.

Mary Gallagher — North London/Willesden, 15–16

ONCE A CATHOLIC MARY O'MALLEY

First performed at The Royal Court Theatre, London in 1977 and set in The Convent of Our Lady of Fatima – a grammar school for girls, and in the streets of Willesden and Harlesden, London, NW10, from September, 1956 to July, 1957.

Mary Gallagher is described as a sensible, attractive, dark-haired fifth-former. In this scene, her boyfriend, Cuthbert, is hearing her through her homework, a scene from *Macbeth*, which has to be learnt for the next day.

Published by Amber Lane Press, Oxford

Act 1, scene 12

Mary Gallagher

'O, full of scorpions is my mind, dear wife.'
'Thou know'st that Banquo and his Fleance lives.' . . . 'There's comfort
yet' . . . er . . . er . . . 'They are assailable.' *(She looks blank.)* Oh yes.
'Then be thou jocund; ere the bat hath flown,
His cloistered flight; ere to black Hecate's summons.' Er . . . the . . . er
. . . the something beetle with his . . . er . . . Tut! Oh, shit! I don't know
it . . . It's got to be word perfect for Mother Peter. Just in case she picks
on me. She's such a crafty old cow. She makes us all learn it but she'll
only pounce on one of us to test it. Whoever she happens to pick on
will have to get up and act it. In front of the whole form. With her. She
always gives herself the part of Lady Macbeth. God, it's so embarrassing. Especially when she starts putting on an English accent and doing
all the fancy gestures. Every time she opens her mouth a spray of spit
comes flying across the classroom. We've all got to go on an outing with
her next Wednesday. To see *Macbeth*. She's taking us up to the Old Vic
. . . Have you ever been there? . . . Lots of people haven't. My Mum and
Dad for a start. Neither of them have ever set foot inside a theatre . . .
They only ever go to the pictures if a film comes round the Coliseum
with a Catholic in the starring role . . . They think an awful lot of
Spencer Tracy. And Bing Crosby. He can do no wrong. And they both
reckon the sun shines right out of Grace Kelly's arse . . . My Dad refuses
to see a film if he thinks the star in it has ever been divorced. And he
gets in a flaming temper if he catches sight of a picture of Lana Turner
in the paper. Just because she's been married a few times. He rips the
picture out of the paper and screws it up and stamps on it. *(in an Irish
accent)* One husband wouldn't satisfy you, ah? Ye two-legged animal!
Aaah!

Lady – American/Southern, 35–40

ORPHEUS DESCENDING TENNESSEE WILLIAMS

First presented at the Martin Beck Theater, New York in 1957 and set in a dry goods store in a small southern town, it is a reworking of the Orpheus and Eurydice story, period 1940. **Lady**, aged between thirty-five and forty, manages the store, while her elderly husband lies upstairs dying of cancer. Worn out from sleepless nights, disillusioned and childless, she meets and is drawn towards Val, a young guitar player, who has just come into town looking for work.

Published by Penguin Books, London

Act 1

Lady

I'd like to be one of those birds . . . If one of those birds ever dies and falls on the ground and you happen to find it, I wish you would show it to me because I think maybe you just imagine there is a bird of that kind of existence. Because I don't think nothing living has ever been that free, not even nearly. Show me one of them birds and I'll say, Yes, God's made one perfect creature! – I sure would give this mercantile store and every bit of stock in it to be that tiny bird the colour of the sky . . . for one night to sleep on the wind and – float! – around under th' – stars . . .

(Jabe knocks on floor. Lady's eyes return to Val.)

– Because I sleep with a son of a bitch who bought me at a fire sale, not in fifteen years have I had a single good dream, not one – oh! – *Shit* . . . I don't know why I'm – telling a stranger – this . . . *(She rings the cashbox open.)* Take this dollar and go eat at the Al-Nite on the highway and come back here in the morning and I'll put you to work. I'll break you in clerking here and when the new confectionery opens, well, maybe I can use you in there. – That door locks when you close it! – But let's get one thing straight . . . I'm not interested in your perfect functions, in fact you don't interest me no more than the air that you stand in. If that's understood we'll have a good working relation, but otherwise trouble! – Of course I know you're crazy, but they's lots of crazier people than you are still running loose and some of them in high positions, too. Just remember. No monkey business with me. Now go. Go eat, you're hungry.

Isabel – America/Southern, 20s

PERIOD OF ADJUSTMENT
TENNESSEE WILLIAMS

First presented at the Helen Hayes Theater in New York City in 1960 and set in a suburban bungalow in a mid-southern city on Christmas Eve. **Isabel**, a young student nurse, has been left on the doorstep of Ralph Bates's bungalow the day after her wedding. Her husband, George, has driven off without a word, taking **Isabel**'s luggage with him. In this scene she pours out her troubles to Ralph, who is trying to watch television.

Published by Dramatists Play Service Inc., New York

Act 1

Isabel

It's like he had St. Vitus Dance, Parkinson's disease, but it isn't Parkinson's disease. It's no disease at all . . . He shakes, that's all. He just shakes. Sometimes you'd think that he was shaking to pieces. *(She crosses to door, hears car, opens it.)* – Was that a car out front? *(He crosses to her.)* No! I've caught a head-cold, darn it. *(Blows nose. She crosses c.)* When I met Mr. George Haverstick – Excuse me, you're watching TV! . . . *(She crosses u. opposite front door.)* I'm so wound up, sitting in silence all day beside my – silent bridegroom, I can't seem to stop talking now, although I – hardly know you. Yes. I met him at Barnes Hospital, the largest hospital in Saint Louis, where I was taking my training as a nurse, he had gone in Barnes instead of the Veterans Hospital because in the Veterans Hospital they couldn't discover any physical cause of this tremor and he thought they just said there wasn't any physical cause in order to avoid having to pay him a physical disability – *(She crosses to chair, sits.)* compensation! – I had him as a patient on the night shift at Barnes Hospital. My, did he keep me running! The little buzzer was never out of his hand. Couldn't sleep under any kind of sedation less than enough to knock an elephant out! – Well, that's where I met George, I was very touched by him, honestly, very, very touched by the boy! I thought he sincerely loved me. I don't suppose another man could see George the way I saw him, so handsome, so afflicted, so afflicted and handsome ... Yes, I have caught a head cold, or am I crying? *(He pulls out handkerchief, gives it to her.)* I guess it's fatigue – exhaustion ... Of course at Barnes he got the same diagnosis, or lack of diagnosis, that he'd gotten at the Vets' Hospital in Korea and Texas and elsewhere, no physical basis for the tremor, perfect physical health, suggested – psychiatry to him! He blew the roof off! You'd think they'd accused him of beating up his grandmother, at least, if not worse! I swear! *(She crosses to door, looks out.)* Mr. Bates, *(Above chair.)* I still have sympathy for him, but it wasn't fair of him not to let me know he'd quit his job until one hour after our marriage. He gave me that information after the wedding, right after the wedding he told me, right on the bridge, Eads Bridge between Saint Louis and East Louis, he said: Little Bit? Take a good look at Saint Louie because it may be your last one! I'm quoting him exactly, those were his words. *(She steps front of chair, sits.)* I don't know why I didn't say drive me right back ... Isn't it strange that I didn't say turn around on the other side of this bridge and drive me right back? I gave up student nursing at a great hospital to marry a man not honest enough to let me know he'd quit his job till an hour after the wedding!

Asma – 17
RETREAT FROM MOSCOW DON TAYLOR

First presented at the New End Theatre, London in 1993 and directed by the author. **Asma**, a seventeen year old Asian girl, anxious to get into university, has been taking extra lessons from Tom, an ex-university lecturer in classics. Her father has refused to pay for any more lessons as he considers it is a waste of money for a girl. He wants her to leave school and is arranging a marriage for her with a business man. In this scene, **Asma** explains how much university means to her and asks Tom if he can possibly defer his fees until she can afford to pay for them herself, as without his help it will be impossible for her to get the necessary grades.

Available by application to Samuel French, London

Act 2

Asma

You see. . . my father has always intended to go back home. He has been here for nearly twenty years, and I am sure he never will: but he's always talking about it. So even after so long, he is not really settled here. My mother speaks very little English, and doesn't go out much except for the shopping. And my father is very shrewd and intelligent, but not an educated man . . . But I am English. I am black, and my parents come from another culture – which they have given me as their most precious gift – but I was born here, I speak like an Englishwoman, I am an Englishwoman. When I go back with my parents – I've been back three times – I feel a stranger there. Well, no. That isn't quite true. In a strange way I feel at home: but that isn't a feeling I want to recognise. It is a different life, brothers, sisters, grandparents, in laws, all together. In England, you live in your separate boxes. My father hates that, but I prefer it. I feel at home here, and I don't want to go back . . . My father thinks I am quite pretty and well educated. He thinks he will make a good marriage for me to a business man over there. Then he will sell up here and go back, go into business with his son-in-law. So I am to leave school at eighteen. I shall be educated enough by then, to make a really good bargaining chip . . . Normally I would be educated as far as I could go: because the higher your qualifications, the better class of marriage you can make. But in my case – well – I think my father already has something fixed up. I'm not certain, but I think so . . . I don't argue with him now. Not if I can avoid it. The big arguments were just after my GCSEs. I love him. I love them both. But I can't do what he wants, and there is no point going on about it. There is a good teacher at school. She thinks I am promising, and she helps me . . . She's not one of my subject teachers. But she has arranged for me about University. Told me what to do . . . I must get three Bs for Leeds, two Bs and a C for Hull . . . I realised I would need extra lessons to get such high grades. My father agreed at first, not really realising what the lessons were. Now he has understood, and has forbidden me to come . . . I need a B in Classics. It isn't like the others in my class. They take it as it comes, some of them want to go to University or Poly very much, but if they don't, it won't be the end of the world. But for me, I must get my grades, because it's my only chance.

Janet – Newcastle, late 20s

RUTHERFORD AND SON GITHA SOWERBY

Written in 1912 and set in the Newcastle Potteries in the same period. It is based on a branch of Githa Sowerby's own family – the Rutherfords – who owned the local glass works. In this scene, **Janet**, unmarried and in her late twenties, is thrown out of the house by her father, because he has discovered her affair with Martin, his Works Manager. Here, she retaliates by telling him her true feelings about him and releases all the pent up emotion and frustrations of an unmarried daughter of that period.

Copies can be obtained from The British Library, London

Act 2

Janet

Me a lady? What do ladies think about, sitting the day long with their hands before them? What have they in their idle hearts? . . . Oh, what more did I want! The women down there know what I wanted . . . with their bairns wrapped in their shawls and their men to come home at night time. I've envied them – envied them their pain, their poorness – the very times they hadn't bread. Theirs isn't the dead empty house, the blank o' the moors; they got something to fight, something to be feared of. They got life, those women we send cans o' soup to out o' pity when their bairns are born. Me a lady! with work for a man in my hands, passion for a man in my heart! I'm common – common . . . Who's risen – which of us? . . . Dick that every one laughs at? John – with his manners? . . . Who's Mary? A little common work-girl – no real gentleman would ha' looked at . . . You think you've made us different by keeping from the people here. We're just the same as they are! Ask the men that work for you – ask their wives that curtsey to us in the road. Do you think they don't know the difference? We're just the same as they are – common, every one of us. It's in our blood, in our hands and faces; and when we marry, we marry common – . . . *(passionately.)* Martin loves me honest. Don't you come near! Don't you touch that! . . . You think I'm sorry you've found out – you think you've done for me when you use shameful words on me and turn me out o' your house. You've let me out o' gaol! Whatever happens to me now, I shan't go on living as I lived here. Whatever Martin's done, he's taken me from you. You've ruined my life, you with your getting on. I've loved in wretchedness, all the joy I ever had made wicked by the fear o' you . . . *(Wildly.)* Who are you? Who are you? A man – a man that's taken power to himself, power to gather people to him and use them as he wills – a man that'd take the blood of life itself and put it into the Works – into Rutherford's. And what ha' you got by it – what? You've got Dick, that you've bullied till he's a fool – John, that's waiting for the time when he can sell what you've done – and you got me – me to take your boots off at night – to well-nigh wish you dead when I had to touch you . . . Now! . . . Now you know!

Mary – London, young/20s

RUTHERFORD AND SON GITHA SOWERBY

Written in 1912 and set in the Newcastle Potteries in the same period. It is based on a branch of Githa Sowerby's own family – the Rutherfords – who owned the local glass works. In this scene, **Mary,** a London girl in her twenties and married to John Rutherford, tells old Mr Rutherford that John has walked out leaving her and her baby son behind. She bargains with Rutherford to let her stay on in the house and bring up her child for the next ten years – then she will hand him over to be brought up in the Rutherford tradition and eventually take John's place in the family business.

Copies may be obtained from The British Library, London

Act 2

Mary

I've lived in your house for nearly three months. *(He turns to look at her.)* Until you came in just now you haven't spoken to me half-a-dozen times. Every slight that can be done without words you've put upon me. There's never a day passed but you've made me feel that I'd no right here, no place . . . Now that I've got to speak to you, I want to say that first – in case you should think I'm going to appeal to you, and in case I should be tempted to do it . . . You can listen – then you can take it or leave it . . . A bargain is where one person has something to sell that another wants to buy. There's no love in it – only money – money that pays for life. I've got something to sell that you want to buy . . . My son. *(Their eyes meet in a long steady look. She goes on deliberately.)* You've lost everything you have in the world. John's gone – and Richard – and Janet. They won't come back. You're alone now and getting old, with no one to come after you. When you die Rutherford's will be sold – somebody'll buy it and give it a new name perhaps, and no one will even remember that you made it. That'll be the end of all your work. Just – nothing. You've thought of that. I've seen you thinking of it as I've sat by and watched you. And now it's come . . . Will you listen? . . . It's for my boy. I want – a chance of life for him – his place in the world. John can't give him that, because he's made so. If I went to London and worked my hardest I'd get twenty-five shillings a week. We've failed. From you I can get what I want for my boy. I want – all the good common things: a good house, good food, warmth. He's a delicate little thing now, but he'll grow strong like other children. I want to undo the wrong we've done him, John and I. If I can. Later on there'll be his schooling – I could never save enough for that. You can give me all this – you've got the power. Right or wrong, you've got the power . . . That's the bargain. Give me what I ask, and in return I'll give you – him. On one condition. I'm to stay on here. I won't trouble you – you needn't speak to me or see me unless you want to. For ten years he's to be absolutely mine, to do what I like with. You mustn't interfere – you mustn't tell him to do things or frighten him. He's mine. For ten years more . . . After that he'll be yours. To train up. For Rutherford's. *(slowly)* There'll be a woman living in the house – year after year, with the fells closed round her. She'll sit and sew at the window and see the chimney flare in the dark; lock up, and give you the keys at night – . . . And I've got him! For ten years. *(They sit silent).* Is it a bargain?

Liz – Yorkshire; young to late 60s

SEPTEMBER IN THE RAIN JOHN GODBER

First presented professionally by the Hull Truck Company in 1984, it is set in Blackpool, where **Liz** and her husband, Jack, are waiting for the bus back home to Yorkshire after their holiday. They are remembering the many holidays spent in Blackpool since they were first married. In this flashback scene they are young again. Jack has just been stung by a jellyfish and Liz is queueing on the beach for an ice-cream.

Published in *John Godber Five Plays*, by Penguin Books, London

Act 1

Liz

(Liz remains downstage. A spotlight picks her out. She is in a queue for an ice-cream. She establishes this by looking front and back.)
Have you seen the length of this queue? That's the trouble when you want an ice-cream, you have to queue for hours to get one. Jack went back to the deckchairs sulking, trying to blame me for what happened. You can guarantee if something is going to happen to someone, it'll happen to Jack. I think I'll get a '99' cornet with a flake in it. Jack'll not want one. He can do without, for being awkward. He usually had a cornet with red sauce on it. Blood on it, he'd say. He can do without. Some of the women, honestly, they look a right sight in bathing costumes, they're not bothered, are they? All the bodies in this queue smell of suntan lotion. Some people buy that stuff that tans whether the sun's out or not. That's bloody daft. Some of the men look quite nice. I suppose I was attracted to them really, standing close up and talking. Mind you they were a bit skinny. You could see their ribs.
'I know, int it a long queue?'
'No, only a week.'
'With my husband.'
'He's just been stung by a jellyfish.'
'No ... I'm not ... ?'
Some blokes'll say owt. I didn't tell Jack, he'd've dislocated their heads for 'em ...
'What?'
'Oh, sorry, can I have a "99" cornet with a flake and one with blood on?'

Magrit – Glaswegian, 30s

THE STEAMIE TONY ROPER

First presented by Wildcat Stage Productions at the Crawford Theatre, Jordanhill College of Education, Glasgow in 1987 and later at the Greenwich Theatre. It is set in a washhouse – The Steamie - on a New Year's Eve in the late fifties in Glasgow. **Magrit**, married and in her thirties, is one of the four Glaswegian women who wash, scrub, have a few drinks and gossip their way through Hogmanay. Towards the end of the play, Andy, the washhouse mechanic, having been heavily plied with scotch by **Magrit** and her friends, enters, swaying unsteadily, and **Magrit** delivers her ironic speech to the audience, addressing her last line to Andy.

From *New Scottish Plays – Scot-Free*, published by Nick Hem Books, London

Act 2

Magrit

(This speech should be done with heavy irony to the audience or she sings 'Isn't it wonderful to be a woman')

Isn't it wonderful tae be a woman. Ye get up at the crack o' dawn and get the breakfast oan, get the weans ready and oot the hoose lookin' as tidy and as well dressed as ye can afford. Then ye see tae the lord high provider and get him oot, then wash up, finish the ironin', tidy the hoose and gie the flair a skite o'er. Then it's oot tae yer ain wee job, mebbe cleanin' offices, servin' in a shop or washin' stairs. Then it's dinner time. Well it is fur everybody else but no us 'cause we don't get dinner. By the time yer oot and run home, cooked something for the weans, yer lucky if you feel like something tae eat. I know I don't and even if I did . . . the dinner hour's finished, so it's back tae yer work; that is efter ye've goat in whatever yer gonnae gie them for their tea, and efter yer finished yer work, ye'r back up . . . cookin' again and they'll tell ye the mince is lumpy . . . or the chips are too warm . . . then they're away oot. The weans tae play . . . the men tae have a drink, cause they need wan . . . the souls . . . efter pittin' in a hard day's graft, so ye've goat the hoose tae yersel' and what dae ye dae, ye tidy up again don't ye? Mer ironin', light the fire, wash the dishes and the pots etc. etc. and then ye sit doon. And what happens . . . ye've just sat doon when the weans come up. 'Gonnae make us a cuppa tea and something tae eat' . . . What dae ye's want tae eat? . . . 'Och anything Ma' . . . D'ye want some o' that soup? . . . 'Naw' A tomato sandwich? . . . 'Naw' . . . A couple o' boiled eggs? . . . 'Naw' . . . A piece 'n spam? . . . 'Naw' . . . Well what d'ye's want? . . . 'Och anything at all'. So ye make them something tae eat then ye sit doon and finally have a wee blaw . . . a very wee blaw . . . cause it's time tae go tae the steamie. Ye go tae the steamie, finish at nine o'clock and get the washin' hame. Ye sort it aw oot . . . and get it put by and then sometimes mebbe take stock of yer life. What are we? . . . skivvies . . . unpaid skivvies . . . in other words we are . . . used . . . but ye think tae yersel', well even if I am being used . . . I don't mind . . . cause I love my family and anyway it's New Year's Eve. I can relax and jist enjoy masel . . . and any minute noo the weans'll be in an ma friends'll be comin' roon wi' black bun, shortbread, dumplin's, a wee refreshment and I can forget aw ma worries even if it's jist for a night and the weans arrive and ye gie them shortbread, sultana cake, ginger wine and there is just one thing missin', the head of the family. The door bell goes, ye open the door, and what is staunin there, ready to make the evening complete . . . that's right . . . your husband, your better half . . . the man who was goin' to make you the happiest woman in the world and (Gently.) what does he look like . . . *that.* (At Andy.)

Josie – London, 30s
STEAMING NELL DUNN

First produced at the Theatre Royal, Stratford, London, in 1981 and then later at the Comedy Theatre, London. It is set in a dilapidated Turkish bath in east London, where five women come to relax and talk through their problems and frustrations. **Josie** is a club hostess aged about thirty-four. In this scene she is talking to Nancy and Jane about working in the topless club. Jane points out that she doesn't need to do this sort of job. Nancy agrees, saying that it is a matter of choice – **Josie** chose to do it. **Josie** retorts that Nancy knows nothing about her situation, the difficulties of finding a decent job and her need for excitement.

Published by Amber Lane Press, Oxford

Act 2, scene 1

Josie

What do you know of it anyway?

(NANCY I know you have to pay for self-respect.)

JOSIE What sort of a job can I get? I'm not even a young girl any more. And I happen to like nice things . . . I like money . . . I don't like wearing 'sensible' shoes and last year's coat and organising other people's lives like a colonel-in-chief. Well, I'm going to tell you something – I don't *want* to be like you. It's boring, it's every day! Boring! Boring! Boring! Do you know why us working-class women have a little bit on the side? Why we spend money on clothes and make-up and shoes when we don't, as you say, 'strictly need them'? We've been brought up to do the shit work and we can't escape from doing the shit work except by finding a man with money and hanging on to him! Anyway, who's to say you've got a better life than me? – I'm not so sure – I've been to South Africa, the Barbados, Tenerife – I've laid beside more pools than you've had hot dinners!

(NANCY On stolen money?)

JOSIE You don't thieve because you don't need to, not because you're any better than I am! I want excitement in my life! I want beautiful clothes, beautiful travelling, cars . . . if I've got to steal them – well, at least I've had them, which is more than I can say for you. Have your drab dreary life and keep your good name if that's what you want. Women should be beautiful things of pleasure. *(She walks away then turns back.)* Do you know what it feels like to go into a library if you don't know your way around . . . and you get looked down on because of your accent? . . . It's a horrible feeling being looked down on – being turned down for job after job because you haven't got the qualifications . . . because you can't spell and you can't speak right . . . and you know in the end all they're going to offer you is cleaning!

(Nancy) *(has stood up)* . . . Please stop!)

JOSIE Why should I stop when you tell me? . . . Who are you . . . Miss Boss? Just because you can spell you think you're Queen of England . . . well, you're not . . . you're just an ordinary woman with a bit of money who's been deserted by her old man – I'm not surprised he left you – you always have to be on top! You pretend different deep down that's how you are – he wanted loving not organizing.

Mavis – London, 40s

STEPPING OUT RICHARD HARRIS

First performed at the Thorndike Theatre, Leatherhead in 1984 and later at the Duke of York's Theatre, London, in the same year. It is set in a Church hall in north London, where a group of women and one man attend a weekly tap dancing class. **Mavis**, in her forties, is an ex-professional dancer who runs the class. In this scene she is rehearsing them for a grand charity show.

Published by Amber Lane Press, Oxford

Act 2, scene 1

Mavis

Okay everyone, let's get on, shall we? It's our first rehearsal, so lots of concentration, yes? . . . *(indicating)* Rose, Sylvia and Andy – we'll take you three at the back – no, Rose in the middle please – then we'll have Maxine, Vera, Lynne and Dorothy – spread yourselves out so you can be seen – but come forward a step, you're crowding – and Geoffrey, let's have you at the front, directly in front of Rose.

(SYLVIA Shame . . .)

MAVIS Okay. So you're standing with your backs to the audience . . . *(She will demonstrate, turning her back to them, as:)* . . . feet apart, and absolutely perfectly still – nothing moving. The curtains or the lights come up or whatever and you stay there, not moving, absolutely static still. For four counts you do absolutely nothing.

[ROSE I like it . . .]

MAVIS On given counts, back line, middle line and Geoffrey turn round and face the front . . . no, you don't move your feet and so your legs are crossed . . .
From there you bring the right arm up, leaving the left arm down, you lift the hat and you hold it high – yes? . . .
On counts three and four, line of four does exactly the same thing but when you turn you leave the right arm down, holding the hat low . . .
Incidentally, there's going to be some fast bouncing around and you

might have bust troubles so wear something good and firm, yes? . . . *(generally)* Right – we'll have the first four bars and make sure the intro is spot on – it's got to be good, it's got to have panache, it's got to have the three T's – what are the three T's? Tits, teeth and tonsils . . . *(demon- strates)* . . . you smile, you stick your chest out, you look like you're enjoying it . . . You've only got two T's, haven't you, Geoffrey? . . . Okay, let's have you in your opening positions and we'll try it again. Quick as you can, please Rose, we've got a lot to get through . . . Dorothy – just a little smaller . . . Sylvia, can we get rid of the gum? I want to see your teeth, not hear them . . . All right? And it's five six seven eight . . . Da da da dada da for nothing . . . Da da da dada da back line . . . Da da da dada da middle line . . . Sway sway Geoffrey! . . . Okay. I think the problem is that when you turn, some of you are a little off balance . . . Right, back into position please and we'll do it again – other way round please, Sylvia – and it's five six seven eight . . . *(demonstrates as:)* Then . . . shuffle ball change, shuffle ball change shuffle ball change, six tap springs and hold. Right – let's try it to the music.

Blanche – American/Southern, 30s

A STREETCAR NAMED DESIRE
TENNESSEE WILLIAMS

First presented at the Barrymore Theater, New York in 1947 and set in the slums of New Orleans. **Blanche** – delicate, uncertain, faded and thirty – has come to live with her sister Stella and husband, Stanley, whom she enrages with her 'airs and graces'. In this scene she is talking to Stanley's friend, Mitch, about the past she is trying to forget.

Published by Samuel French, London

Scene 6

Blanche

He was a boy, just a boy, when I was a very young girl. When I was sixteen, I made the discovery – love. All at once and much, much too completely. It was like you suddenly turned a blinding light on something that had always been half in shadow, that's how it struck the world for me. But I was unlucky. Deluded. There was something different about the boy, a nervousness, a softness and tenderness which wasn't like a man's, although he wasn't the least bit effeminate-looking – still – that thing was there . . . He came to me for help. I didn't know that. I didn't find out anything till after our marriage when we'd run away and come back and all I knew was I'd failed him in some mysterious way and wasn't able to give the help he needed but couldn't speak of! He was in the quicksands and clutching at me – but I wasn't holding him out, I was slipping in with him! I didn't know that. I didn't know anything except I loved him unendurably but without being able to help him or help myself. Then I found out. In the worst of all possible ways. By coming suddenly into a room that I thought was empty – which wasn't empty, but had two people in it . . . Afterwards we pretended that nothing had been discovered. Yes, the three of us drove out to Moon Lake Casino, very drunk and laughing all the way . . . We danced the Varsouviana! Suddenly in the middle of the dance the boy I had married broke away from me and ran out of the casino. A few moments later – a shot! . . . I ran out – all did – all ran and gathered about the terrible thing at the edge of the lake! I couldn't get near for the crowding. Then somebody caught my arm. 'Don't go any closer! Come back! You don't want to see!' See? See what! Then I heard voices say – Allan! Allan! The Grey boy! He'd stuck the revolver into his mouth, and fired – so that the back of his head had been – blown away!
(She sways and covers her face)
It was because – on the dance-floor – unable to stop myself – I'd suddenly said – 'I know! I know! You disgust me . . .' And then the searchlight which had been turned on the world was turned off again and never for one moment since has there been any light that's stronger than this – kitchen – candle . . .

Gail – Set somewhere in England, 16–17

TEECHERS JOHN GODBER

First performed by the Hull Truck Company at the Edinburgh Festival in 1987 and set in a school hall, with a wooden stage, desks and chairs. School leavers, Salty, Hobby and **Gail** are presenting a play about life at Whitewall High – described as a comprehensive school somewhere in England, with its fair share of problems. All three play several different characters, sometimes acting as narrators. Here **Gail** plays 'Bobby Moxon' – the cock of Whitewall High – known to all and sundry as – 'Oggy Moxon'.

Published in *John Godber Five Plays*, by Penguin Books

Act 1

Gail

Oggy Moxon's speech about being hard: I'm Oggy Moxon . . . We said you'd have to use your imaginations. I'm Oggy, I'm as hard as nails, as toe-capped boots I'm hard, as marble in a church, as concrete on your head I'm hard. As calculus I'm hard. As learning Hebrew is hard, then so am I. Even Basford knows I'm rock, his cane wilts like an old sock. And if any teachers in the shitpot school with their degrees and bad breath lay a finger on me, God be my judge, I'll have their hides. And if not me, our Nobby will be up to this knowledge college in a flash. All the female flesh fancy me in my five-o-ones, no uniform for me never. From big Mrs Crimes to pert Miss Prime I see their eyes flick to my button holed flies. And they know like I that no male on this staff could satisfy them like me, cos I'm hard all the time. Last Christmas dance me and Miss Prime pranced to some bullshit track and my hand slipped down her back, and she told me she thought that I was great, I felt that arse, that schoolboy wank, a tight-buttocked, Rebok-footed, leggy-arse . . . I touched that and heard her sigh . . . for me. And as I walk my last two terms through these corridors of sickly books and boredom, I see grown men flinch and fear. In cookery one day my hands were all covered with sticky paste, and in haste I asked pretty Miss Bell if she could get for me an hanky from my pockets, of course she would, a student on teaching practice – wanting to help, not knowing my pockets had holes and my underpants were in the wash. 'Oh, no,' she yelped, but in truth got herself a thrill, and has talked of nothing else these last two years. Be warned, when Oggy Moxon is around get out your cigs . . . And lock up your daughters . . .

Sarah Casey – Irish/West of Ireland, young

THE TINKER'S WEDDING J. M. SYNGE

Written in about 1902 and not performed until 1909, it is set at a village roadside after nightfall. A tinker, Michael Byrne, is working beside a stick fire near to a chapel gate. **Sarah Casey**, a young tinker girl, is urging him to finish making her wedding ring, and hoping she can waylay the Priest and persuade him to marry them. When the Priest does arrive, he wants nothing to do with the likes of **Sarah Casey**.

Published by Methuen, London

Act 1

Sarah Casey

(Coming in on right, eagerly)
We'll see his reverence this place, Michael Byrne, and he passing backward to his house to-night . . . *(sharply)* And it'll be small joy for yourself if you aren't ready with my wedding ring. *(She goes over to him.)* Is it near done this time, or what way is it at all? . . . *(sitting down beside him and throwing sticks on the fire)* If it's the divil's job, let you mind it, and leave your speeches that would choke a fool . . . springtime is a queer time, and it's queer thoughts maybe I do think at whiles . . . *(teasingly)* It's at the dawn of day I do be thinking I'd have a right to be going off to the rich tinkers do be travelling from Tibradden to the Tara Hill; for it'd be a fine life to be driving with young Jaunting Jim, where there wouldn't be any big hills to break the back of you, with walking up and walking down . . . *(She takes the ring from him and tries it on.)* It's making it tight you are, and the edges sharp on the tin . . . *(giving it back to him)* Fix it now, and it'll do, if you're wary you don't squeeze it again . . . *(looking out right)* There's someone coming forward from the doctor's door . . . It's a big boast of a man with a long step on him and a trumpeting voice. It's his reverence, surely; and if you have the ring down, it's a great bargain we'll make now and he after drinking his glass . . . *(tidying herself, in great excitement)* Let you be sitting here and keeping a great blaze, the way he can look on my face; and let you seem to be working, for it's great love the like of him have to talk of work . . .

(The Priest comes in on right; she comes forward in front of him.) In a very plausible voice. Good evening, your reverence. It's a grand fine night, by the grace of God . . . It's Sarah Casey I am, your reverence, the Beauty of Ballinacree, and it's Michael Byrne is below in the ditch . . . We were thinking maybe we'd have a right to be getting married; and we were thinking it's yourself would marry us for not a halfpenny at all; for you're a kind man, your reverence, a kind man with the poor . . . *(pleadingly, taking money from her pocket)* Wouldn't you have a little mercy on us, your reverence? *(Holding out money.)* Wouldn't you marry us for a half a sovereign, and it a nice shiny one with a view on it of the living king's mamma? . . . *(whining)* It's two years we are getting that bit, your reverence, with our pence and our halfpence and an odd three-penny bit; and if you don't marry us now, himself and the old woman, who has a great drouth, will be drinking it tomorrow in the fair *(she puts her apron to her eyes, half sobbing)*, and then I won't be married any time, and I'll be saying till I'm an old woman: 'It's a cruel and wicked thing to be bred poor.'

Woman – American/Massachusetts, middle-aged
VERONICA'S ROOM IRA LEVIN

First presented at the Music Box Theater in 1973 in New York and set in a room in the Brabissant mansion near Boston, Massachusetts. Susan, a young college student, is lured back to the Brabissant mansion by a 'Man' and '**Woman**' pretending to be a sweet little old Irish couple, and is persuaded to dress up as 'Veronica' who died in 1935. She is locked in an upstairs room, and the **Woman**, now speaking in her normal Massachusetts accent, insists that Susan really is Veronica and that the year is 1935, not 1973.

Published by Samuel French, London

Act 2

Woman

Why do you think you're kept in this room? . . . If you had TB . . . you would be in a sanatorium . . . If you had TB, your door wouldn't be locked, and your windows wouldn't be barred. *With wrought iron costing six hundred and fifty dollars* . . . If you had TB, it would be an enormous improvement . . . You're kept here – because you *killed* Cissie . . . Does that 'ring a bell'? Does that 'penetrate the miasma'?
(The Girl *shakes her head, staring at the* Woman*)*
One afternoon when you were fifteen years old – Friday, November twenty-first, nineteen thirty, to be precise – you hit her on the head with a shovel, more than once, down in the cellar, and you hauled her into the coal bin, and put her beneath the chute. It was the day and time when a delivery was coming. It came. Five tons. I found her only a little while later; I had seen her go down there after you, and one of her legs was sticking out. I found *you* up *here*, scrub-a-dub-dubbing. You hadn't quite finished yet, unfortunately for you . . . Unfortunately for *me*, your father decided – *(a nod to the* Man*)* – for his own pea-brained reasons – *(and back to the* Girl*)* – not to hand you over to the police. And he has since spent more than twenty thousand dollars *keeping* our little secret. Five thousand dollars to Dr Harvey, for overlooking the shovel marks – do you remember Dr Harvey, before Dr Simpson?

(The Girl shakes her head)
Another five thousand dollars to the coroner, ditto, ditto, ditto. Two thousand dollars to someone at Devereaux, for keeping you on the records through graduation, though we took you out and put you here. You do remember Devereaux, don't you?
(The Girl shakes her head)
No? I could have sworn you did. *(She sings, to the tune of 'Buffalo Girls')*

> Devereaux girls gonna stand up and fight,
> Gonna stand up and fight,
> Gonna stand up and fight . . .

A thousand dollars every Christmas to John and Maureen – which, I suppose, is why in nineteen seventy-three they'll be dining in restaurants; five hundred every Christmas to Henrietta; the same to Dr Simpson, who wondered, of course, why we have a daughter in *stir*; and sundry miscellaneous expenditures – the grillwork, the jigsaw puzzles, the occasional broken mirrors and windows. *(She lifts her wrist, and points)* The Band-Aids . . . *That* is reality, Veronica. You killed Cissie. That's why you're kept here in nineteen thirty-five and that's why you'll be kept here in nineteen thirty-six and in nineteen thirty-seven, and in nineteen thirty-eight and in nineteen seventy-three, and in every year until you die. I swore that to Cissie, when I kissed her in her coffin. *(She moves away)*
(The Girl stands shaking her head weakly. The Man sits down again on the foot of the chaise)
(Turning to the Girl) And you can stop dropping those notes out of the window; Conrad won't help you. *He* feels the same way *we* do. When *we* die, he'll keep you locked here. *He* swore that to *me*, on the Bible . . .
Now what were you saying about meeting us in a restaurant?

Claire – 35, American

WHOSE LIFE IS IT ANYWAY BRIAN CLARK

NEW VERSION – FEMALE

This new version starring Kim Cattrall was produced at the Comedy Theatre, London in January 2005.

Following an accident, **Claire** is paralysed and lying completely still in her bed. She is incapable of living outside the hospital. The medical staff are committed to keeping her alive, but she claims that she has the right to die and wants to discharge herself from their care. She hires a solicitor, Helen Hill, to represent her. The hospital counter by having her committed under the mental health act, but **Claire** is determined to fight her case to be allowed to die. Afer studying the psychiatric reports, Helen agrees to take the case to court.

A video link camera is connected from the Court to **Claire**'s room and in this final scene, the Judge, Mrs Justice Millhouse, comes to the hospital to question **Claire**. She points out that a desperately distressed person might not be making a reasonable choice. Is it a reasonable choice that made **Claire** decide to die?

Published by Amber Lane Press, Charlbury, Oxfordshire.

Claire

As you said, my lady, that is the question to be decided . . . The best part of my life was, I suppose, my work. The most valuable asset that I had for that was my imagination. It's just a shame that my mind wasn't paralysed along with my body. Because my imagination – which was my most precious possession – has become my enemy. And it tortures me with thoughts of what might have been and of what might be to come. I can feel my mind slowly breaking up. For example, men. I loved what they were, the look of them, the way they thought, the smell of them . . . Now I dread it when they come into the room because I loathe the way they make me feel. You know, I am filled with absolute outrage that you, who have no connection with me whatever, has the right to condemn me to a life of torment because you can't see the pain. There's no blood and there's no screaming so you can't see it. But if you saw a mutilated animal on the side of the road, you'd shoot it. Well, I'm only asking that you show me the same mercy you'd show an animal. But I'm not asking you to commit an act of violence, just take me somewhere and leave me. And if you don't, then you come back here in five years and see what a piece of work you did today.

Mother – Rural, 60s

THE WITCH OF EDMONTON WILLIAM ROWLEY, THOMAS DEKKER AND JOHN FORD

A tragicomedy written in 1621 and often performed at The Cockpit in Drury Lane. Old **Mother Sawyer** – the Witch – has sold her soul to the devil, who appeared to her in the shape of a black dog, so that she might be revenged on all those that harmed her. In this scene, she is at the height of her powers, and although the villagers have just set fire to her cottage, takes great delight in taunting the lecherous Sir Arthur, and the Justice who has been brought in to question her.

Act 4, scene 2

Mother

A witch? Who is not?
Hold not that universal name in scorn then.
What are your painted things in princes' courts,
Upon whose eyelids lust sits, blowing fires
To burn men's souls in sensual, hot desires,
Upon whose naked paps a lecher's thought
Acts sin in fouler shapes than can be wrought? . . .
These by enchantments can whole lordships change
To trunks of rich attire, turn ploughs and teams
To Flanders mares and coaches, and huge trains
Of servitors to a French butterfly.
Have you not city witches who can turn
Their husbands' wares, whole standing shops of wares,
To sumptuous tables, gardens of stol'n sin.
In one year wasting what scarce twenty win?
Are not these witches?
Why then on me,
Or any lean old beldam? Reverence once
Had wont to wait on age; now an old woman,
Ill-favour'd grown with years, if she be poor,
Must be call'd bawd or witch. Such so abus'd
Are the coarse witches; t'other are the fine
Spun for the devil's own wearing . . .
She on whose tongue a whirlwind sits to blow
A man out of himself, from his soft pillow,
To lean his head on rocks and fighting waves,
Is not that scold a witch? The man of law
Whose honeyed hopes the credulous client draws –
As bees to tinkling basins – to swarm to him
From his own hive, to work the wax in his –
He is no witch, not he! . . .
Dare any swear I ever tempted maiden,
With golden hooks flung at her chastity,
To come and lose her honour, and being lost
To pay not a denier for't? Some slaves have done it.
Men-witches can, without the fangs of law
Drawing once one drop of blood, put counterfeit pieces
Away for true gold.

Tina – young

THE WOMAN BEFORE
RICHARD SCHIMMELPFENNIG
TRANSLATED BY DAVID TUSHINGHAM

First performed at the Royal Court Theatre, London in 2005.

Frank and his wife, Claudia, are moving house. As they are packing, a woman arrives on the doorstep and announces that she and Frank were lovers 24 years ago and she has come to claim him back. Meanwhile their son, Andi, is saying goodbye to his girlfriend, **Tina**, whom he knows he will never see again.

The action shifts backs and forwards between scenes, often repeating part of the previous dialogue. It is described as a 'flight of fancy' – but ends on an unexpected and sinister twist.

In this scene, set towards the end of the play, **Tina** and Andi have said their goodbyes and Andi has gone back into the house. **Tina** waits outside, expecting him to come out again. Eventually she knocks at the door and Frank tells her Andi never returned to the house. He thought Andi was at *her* house. **Tina** goes back to the bank where they said goodbye. She stands staring at the house, certain that Andi will come out again.

Published by Oberon Modern Plays, London

Tina

I can't leave – I can't leave there, I can't.

Brief pause.

I can't leave the place where Andi must be and isn't. Where can he have gone? He has to be there but he isn't there. I run back and forth in panic, I wait at the top of the bank where we always used to meet, where we –

Brief pause.

Where we threw the stones, I sit there, alone, I even throw stones, at nothing, because no one comes in and no one goes out, except for Andi's mother who goes into the building and then I walk around again, back and forth, up and down, eventually I go all the way round the building, from the back, behind the building, you can see into Andi's parents' bedroom, with the fitted wardobes and the big bed and suddenly Claudia, Andi's mother staggers into the room, she's surprised or maybe even confused, she's got a plastic bag in her hands, I get the feeling I've seen that bag before.

Brief pause.

She's still standing in the doorway, undecided, uncertain, only then does she go into the room, holding the bag, there's something she doesn't understand, that much I can see. She reaches inside the bag, it seems to be empty from out here, at least that's what it looks like through the window and the moment, the moment she reaches inside the bag, at least that's what it looks like through the window, her fingers, her hands, her arms suddenly catch fire. There in her bedroom the woman catches fire all over, she's burning, her whole body is burning, she burns so quickly so horribly – she doesn't even seem to be able to scream – I scream, I scream as loud as I can but who's going to hear me – and then Andi's father appears in the doorway, he sees his wife on fire with the molten remains of the bag in her hand and he stands there not moving until he vanishes from the doorway again. I run. The removal van's coming down the street and stops in front of the building. Where's Andi –

more ideas *for* speeches

Judith – Irish/Donegal; aged late 30s

ARISTOCRATS BRIAN FRIEL

First performed at the Abbey Theatre, Dublin in 1979 and set in Ballybeg Hall, County Donegal, where the O'Donnell family have gathered together for a wedding.

Judith cares little for her appearance and is dressed in working clothes. In this scene, Eamon reminds her of the time she promised to marry him. Why did she change her mind? Judith ignores his question. Her speech becomes tense and deliberate as she describes how her days are filled looking after her invalid father.

Published by Gallery Books

Act II

START: 'We manage because . . .
TO: and I enjoy baking . . .

CUT TO: 'So that apart . . .
TO: 'It's used very little anyhow . . .

CUT TO: 'And I have Willie . . .
TO: take him for granted . . .

CUT TO: 'Listen to me, Eamon . . .
END: Keep out of it. Now. Altogether. Please.'

Sophie – English, aged 24

ARTIST DESCENDING A STAIRCASE
TOM STOPPARD

First produced in the theatre at The King's Head, London in 1988. It examines the relationship between three artists – Beauchamp, Donner and Martello – from 1914 to the present day, and their friendship with **Sophie**, a young blind girl who becomes Beauchamp's lover.

In a flashback to 1922, **Sophie** is alone in their flat. She has just discovered that Beauchamp is leaving her behind when he moves to Chelsea, and that Donner, known as 'Mouse', who has always loved her, is staying on to look after her. The situation is unbearable, and at the end of this scene she falls/throws herself from the window onto the flagstones below.

Published in *Four Plays for Radio*, by Faber & Faber, London

P 151
START: 'I feel blind again . . .

TO: . . . Oh no, there is no way now – I won't – I won't – I won't – no, I won't . . . !'

Note: Sophie *also has two excellent speeches on pages 130 and 134.*

Lena – South African/Cape Coloured; 50s

BOESMAN AND LENA ATHOL FUGARD

First performed at the Rhodes University Little Theatre, Grahamstown, South Africa, in 1969.

Lena is trudging barefoot behind her 'man', Boesman. Their home has been razed to the ground that morning by the 'whiteman' and she carries her bundle of possessions on her head. (She has been reduced to a dumb, animal-like submission by the weight of her burden and the long walk behind them.) She berates Boesman for taking her the long way round.

From *Selected Plays*, Oxford University Press

Act I

START: 'Why didn't we come the short way then? . . .
CUT TO: 'It didn't used to feel . . .
TO: Still out there walking'

CUT TO: 'All you knew was to load up our things . . .
TO: I would have gone, Boesman . . .

CUT TO: 'They also laughed . . .
END: Ten cents worth of bruises.'

Maggie – Irish/Donegal; 30s

DANCING AT LUGHNASA BRIAN FRIEL

First performed in 1990 at the Abbey Theatre, Dublin.

The play is set in 1936 and it is harvest time in County Donegal. **Maggie** lives in the village of Ballybeg with her four sisters and her brother, Father Jack, a priest recently repatriated from Africa. **Maggie** is in the kitchen making soda bread and talking to her sisters. Kate mentions that she has just met a friend of hers, Bernie O'Donnell, in the post office. This reminds **Maggie** of the dancing contest she and Bernie went in for in Ardstraw.

Published by Faber & Faber, London

Act I

START: 'When I was sixteen . . .

END: 'I mean they must have been blind drunk, those judges, whoever they were . . .'

Joanna – mid-40s
DISPOSING OF THE BODY HUGH WHITMORE

First presented at the Hampstead Theatre Club, London, in 1999.

Henry Preece and his wife, Angela, have just moved out of London and into a cottage at Stoke Amberley. Their nearest neighbours are a married couple of similar age, **Joanna** and Alexander. When Alexander hears that Henry is writing a book, he suggests that his wife might do some secretarial work for him. Over the next two months the working relationship develops into a passionate affair.

In this early scene, Henry invites **Joanna** out to lunch. Over a bottle of wine they discuss his book. **Joanna** remarks that he makes the '30s and '40s seem such a happy time. This prompts Henry to talk about his parents, and **Joanna** tells him how she had dreamt about them the other night

Published by Amber Lane Press, Charlbury, Oxfordshire

Act I

START: 'I dreamt about them . . .
TO: . . . New York.'

CUT TO: 'Dreams are very important . . .
TO: some connection'

CUT TO: (My father) 'died five years ago . . .
TO: I want him to forgive me.'

CUT TO: 'He loved Eastbourne. . .
TO: Sorry.'

END ON: 'He knew I was ashamed of him.'

Note I have added in (My father) so that the speech refers back to Henry's previous remark.

Hester – White South African, 30s
HELLO AND GOODBYE ATHOL FUGARD

First produced at the Library Theatre, Johannesburg in 1965 and set in Johnny Smit's kitchen in Port Elizabeth. A definitive performance, directed by the author, was first presented at the Space, Cape Town in 1974 and subsequently at the Riverside Studios, London in 1978.

Hester, a poor South African white, earning her living by prostitution, returns home after a long absence. In this opening scene she is talking to her brother, Johnnie, about her journey and trying to put into words her feelings about coming back.

From *Selected Plays*, Athol Fugard, Oxford University Press

Act I
START: 'Then shut up and listen!
TO: I got frightened . . .

CUT TO: '. . . Maybe frightened is wrong . . .
TO: . . . remembering like never before . . .

CUT TO: 'So then I said, No, this isn't wise . . .
END: I was ready to do it. 'Strue's God!'

Merteuil – set in Paris; 30s

LES LIAISONS DANGEREUSES
CHRISTOPHER HAMPTON

First produced by the Royal Shakespeare Company at The Other Place, Stratford-upon-Avon in 1985 and later at the Barbican, London in 1986.

The action takes place in various salons, bedrooms, hotels and chateaux in and around Paris in the 1780s. In this scene, the **Marquise de Merteuil** plots yet another of her many intrigues, with her confidant and ex-lover, the Vicomte de Valmont.

Published by Faber & Faber, London

Act I scene 4
START: 'Well, as a matter of fact . . .
TO: I'm sure you will . . . '

CUT TO: 'I've become extremely thick with little Cecile . . .
TO: altogether delicious . . .

CUT TO: 'She and Danceny . . .
END: I wished I was.'

Mrs Betterton – 50s

PLAYHOUSE CREATURES APRIL DE ANGELIS

First performed at the Haymarket Studios, Leicester in 1993 and later that year at the Lyric Studio, Hammersmith.

It is set in 1669 in Restoration London and follows the lives of five actresses, one of them the famous Nell Gwyn, and their struggle against the threat of poverty and pestilence. Now they are demanding shares in the theatre company, and in this scene, **Mrs Betterton**, a renowned actress in her day and the wife of Actor Manager, Thomas Betterton, stands on stage trying to put their case to her husband, whom we never see, but who is 'supposedly' sitting at the back of the auditorium.

Published by Samuel French, London

Act II scene 2

START: 'Thomas? Thomas? It is the matter we discussed at breakfast. You remember . . .

END: 'Indeed, Thomas, you are the one that's partial to cheese.'

useful addresses

The Actors' Theatre School,
32 Exeter Road
London NW2 4SB
tel: 020 8450 0371
fax: 020 8450 1057

American Academy of Dramatic
  Art
120 Madison Avenue
New York
NY 10016
tel: 212-686 9244

The British Library,
96 Euston Road
London NW1 2DB
tel: 020 7412 7000

Drama Studio London
Grange Court
1 Grange Road
London W5 5QN
tel: 020 8579 3897

London Academy of Music and
Dramatic Art (LAMDA)
155 Talgarth Road
London W14 9DA
tel: 020 8834 0500

Offstage Theatre and Film
  Bookshop,
37 Chalk Farm Road
London NW1 8AJ
tel: 020 7485 4996
fax: 020 7916 8046

Royal Academy of Dramatic Art
62/64 Gower Street
London WC1E 6ED
tel: 020 7636 7076

Victoria Library
Via Westminster Library
160 Buckingham Palace Road
London SW1 9UD
tel: 020 7641 4292

copyright holders

The following have kindly granted permission for the reprinting of copyright material.

Antigone by Sophocles. From *Three Theban Plays* by Sophocles, translated by Robert Fagles. Translation copyright © 1982 by Robert Fagles. Used by permission of Viking Penguin, a division of Penguin Books USA Inc.

Bar Mitzvah Boy by Jack Rosenthal. Extract from *Bar Mitzvah Boy* by Jack Rosenthal © 1978. Mistlodge Ltd 1978. All rights whatsoever in this play are strictly reserved and application for performance etc., should be made before rehearsal to Casarotto Ramsay Ltd, National House, 60–66 Wardour Street, London W1V 3HP. No performance may be given unless a licence has been obtained.

Blood Relations by Sharon Pollock. *Blood Relations* by Sharon Pollock from *Blood Relations and Other Plays.* © Reprinted by permission of NeWest Publishers Limited, Edmonton.

Break Away by Dameon Garnett. Reproduced by permission of Oberon Books Ltd.

Breezeblock Park by Willy Russell. © 1978 by Willy Russell published by Samuel French Ltd. All rights whatsoever in this play are strictly reserved and application for performance etc., should be made before rehearsal to Casarotto Ramsay Ltd, National House, 60–66 Wardour Street, London W1V 3HP. No performance may be given unless a licence has been obtained.

Daughters of Venice by Don Taylor. © 1992 by Don Taylor published by Samuel French Ltd. All rights whatsoever in this play are strictly reserved and application for performance etc., should be made before rehearsal to Micheline Steinberg Associates, 104 Great Portland Street, London W1W 6PE. No performance may be given unless a licence has been obtained.

Death and the Maiden by Ariel Dorfman, copyright © 1990, 1994 Ariel Dorfman. Reprinted by permission of the publisher: www.nickhern books.co.uk.

Death of a Salesman by Arthur Miller. Extract from *Death of a Salesman* by Arthur Miller. Copyright © 1949 by Arthur Miller. Reproduced by permission of the author c/o Rogers, Coleridge & White Ltd, 20 Powis Mews, London W11 1JN in association with International Creative Management, New York.

The Devil's Disciple by George Bernard Shaw. Reprinted by permission of The Society of Authors on behalf of the Estate of Bernard Shaw. Published by Penguin.

Diff'rent by Eugene O'Neill. From *Collected Plays of Eugene O'Neill*, published by Jonathan Cape. Copyright © 1921 and renewed 1949 by Eugene O'Neill. Reprinted by permission of The Random House Group Ltd.

Have You Seen Zandile? by Gcina Mhlophe, Maralin Vanrenen and Thembi Mtshali. Published by Heinemann Copyright © 1988 Reproduced by permission of Heinemann.

His Dark Materials – Part Two by Nicolas Wright, based on the novels by Philip Pullman, copyright © 2003, 2004 Somerset West Limited. Reprinted by permission of the publisher: www.nickhern books.co.uk.

In the Bag by Wang Xiaoli in a version by Ronan O'Donnell, copyright © 2005 Wang Xiaoli and Ronan O'Donnell. Reprinted by permission of the publisher: www.nickhernbooks.co.uk.

Ivanov by Anton Chekhov. Short extract from Act IV (p114) from *Ivanov* from *Plays* by Anton Chekhov, translated by Elisaveta Fen (Penguin Classics, 1951). Copyright © Elisaveta Fen, 1951, 1954. Reproduced by permission of Penguin Books Ltd.

Jitney by August Wilson, copyright © 1997–2000 the Estate of the late August Wilson. Reprinted by permission of the publisher: www.nickhernbooks.co.uk.

The Kid by Michael Gow. From *The Kid* by Michael Gow, published by The Currency Press. Reproduced by permission of Shanahan Management Pty Ltd.

The Lady from the Sea by Henrik Ibsen. Extract from pp 313–314 from Act V from *The Lady from the Sea* by Henrik Ibsen, translated by Peter Watts (Penguin Classics, 1965). Copyright © Peter Watts, 1965. Reproduced by permission of Penguin Books Ltd.